LOOKING
GOOD
ON
PAPER

LOOKING GOOD ON PAPER

How to create eye-catching reports, proposals, memos, and other business documents

GARRETT SODEN

amacom

American Management Association

New York • Atlanta • Boston • Chicago • Kansas City • San Francisco • Washington, D.C.
Brussels • Mexico City • Tokyo • Toronto

Library of Congress Cataloging-in-Publication Data

Soden, Garrett.
    Looking good on paper: how to create eye-catching
    reports, proposals, memos, and other business
    documents / Garrett Soden.
            p.   cm.
    Includes bibliographic references (p. 119).
    ISBN 0-8144-7858-1
    1. Business report writing. 2. Printing, Practical—
Layout. I. Title.
HF5719.S65 1995
651.7\4—dc20   94-27096
                                                     CIP

Printing number

10 9 8 7 6 5 4 3 2

Contents

The purpose of document design is not to decorate, but to get your ideas into the mind of your reader as efficiently as possible—in other words, to persuade your reader. This introduction tells how the persuasion process works and why visual design is essential to that process.

Because design is a form of communication, you must be clear about what you are communicating, who you are communicating it to, what method of communication will work best, and what you expect from your reader as a result. All this should happen before you begin the actual design of your document.

27 Design As You Write

When you write, you are translating your ideas into words; as soon as you put these words on paper you are designing, because you are transferring them to a visual medium. By understanding how to apply visual cues to your composition as you write, you will create a solid foundation on which you can build a visually powerful document.

43 Use Fonts Well

The words of your document are made visible through the fonts you choose and are made understandable by the way you use those fonts. Different fonts communicate different emotional tones; their size and arrangement on the page make them readable or not. In this section you will learn how to analyze the emotional quality of a font and how to arrange text to ensure readability.

77 **Guide Your Reader**

The final step in document design is to combine all the material you have into an integrated, visual whole, one that leads your reader through your ideas and communicates them with maximum impact.

Preface and Acknowledgments

THIS BOOK IS DIFFERENT from other books on publication design and desktop publishing because it is about business. It is also different because it is not about a particular software program, it doesn't show unexplained before and after examples, it doesn't offer a random list of tips, and it doesn't feature beautiful layouts that are beyond the skill of the average person. There are thousands of aspects of publication design—its aesthetics, its history, its social impact—so many, in fact, that most books get lost following one favorite tangent or the other and are useless to the person who just wants to know how to get a point across visually.

Instead, I have written a book that does two things. First, it presents a direct and systematic approach to document design. I've restricted my advice to a short set of simple, definite rules. Publication experts, no doubt, could find exceptions to every one, but if you are not an expert, learning the rules will serve you well, because they will show you how to communicate visually.

Second, it covers only the skills you need if you are not a designer and don't want to become one. If you want to become a designer, there are many schools and hundreds of books that dwell on the fine points. In this book you'll find succinct information for the average businessperson with a word processor or desktop publishing system who needs to improve the look of his documents.

My model has been Strunk and White's classic on English composition, *The Elements of Style*. Like Strunk and White, I've tried to be clear and concise and to illustrate most rules with examples. You can use the guidelines to boost the persuasive power of your memos, letters, and reports and to learn how to design sophisticated publications such as newsletters, magazines, and advertisements with professional results.

The ideas in this book were gathered over twenty years, through my experience as a publication designer and director of corporate communications and through my own study of the subject. Aside from Strunk and White, there were also authors of design books who set me on the right path—in particular, Jan White, James Craig, Ruari McLean, Stanley Morrison, Beatrice Warde, and Allen Hurlburt. I am in their debt.

I would also like to thank Martin Weinberger, who gave me my first job in design and allowed me to experiment on many a Saturday issue of the *Claremont Courier*; Rose Marie Fuller, who gave me room to refine my skills on all manner of publications; Tom Colvin, Floyd Lawrence, and Rebecca Rona, Occidental College colleagues with whom I explored publication design in the academic world and Jan Baird, who gave me a great opportunity to apply some of the theories in this book to real-world corporate problems.

I also owe a great deal to my student interns at Occidental College, all of whom helped me learn how to explain design, and who constantly renewed my own enthusiasm for the subject. They include Mary Tesluk, Tim Simmons, Mimi Ahn, Kait Campbell, and Sam McKelvey.

I would also like to thank Janice Ridenour, a former student who became a colleague and a friend; she is a fine designer and writer who understands communication design and who has taught me much.

Finally, endless appreciation is due my family: my daughter Jordan Seider, who lets me use the computer once in a while; my wife, Denise K. Seider, always my first editor, principal b.s. detector, and soul mate without peer; and my parents, Walter and Enid Soden, who taught me how to apply logical reasoning to subjects that would seem to resist rationality of any kind.

Introduction:
The Hidden Power of Document Design

Before computers, most business documents looked like this. If yours still do, you're neglecting a powerful new set of communication tools.

NOT LONG AGO, people in business didn't have to worry much about designing their documents because they didn't have that option. You simply rolled a sheet of paper into your typewriter (or asked your secretary to) and typed up your memo, report, or resume. Very few documents called for the time and expense of design, typesetting, and printing. The playing field was level. No one worried about a document's looks because they all looked pretty much the same.

Computers have changed all that, of course. Now anyone with a decent word processor and printer has a new set of powerful communication tools: thousands of fonts to choose from, unlimited font sizes, the ability to put type in columns, boxes, or tables, and much more.

Notice that I call these *communication* tools, not artistic tools or decorative tools. You can use these tools to simply decorate your document, but that's like using spreadsheet software to organize a laundry list. If you know how, you can instead use these tools to boost your communication to a far higher level of effectiveness. The tools are there—probably on your desk right now—whether you choose to use their power or not. This book is about choosing to use that power.

When used well, good document design will reveal

your thinking. If your thinking is clear, that will be shown; if it's muddled, that will be shown too. There is no font that will put a good face on a bad idea.

Assuming your thinking is sound, the great advantage visual tools give you is the ability to put your ideas into the mind of your reader faster and more completely than your competitors. That makes it more likely that your ideas will be shared and talked about. Other things being equal, if your good idea is understood first, it will be put into action first. Let's take a closer look at this process.

Designed to Persuade

In their book *Age of Propaganda* (W. H. Freeman & Company), psychologists Anthony Pratkanis and Elliot Aronson summarize the persuasion model based on the classic work of researcher Carl Hovland and his colleagues*:

1. The message must attract the recipient's attention.
2. The arguments in the message must be understood and comprehended.
3. The recipient must learn the arguments contained in the message and come to accept them as true.
4. We act on this learned knowledge and beliefs when there is an incentive to do so.

The four stages of persuasion

1. Attract attention to your message.

Each of these stages can be enhanced by good document design. In fact, good design can mean the difference between a document that successfully persuades and one that doesn't. Let's look at the critical role design plays at each step of the process:

1. *The message must attract the recipient's attention.* Most people realize that a well-designed document will attract more attention than a poorly designed one. But look closely at the statement. It says the *message* must

attract attention—not the document. People often add wild fonts, big headlines, or irrelevant graphics to their work to try to "make it stand out from the crowd." It well may, but not for the right reasons. If your design does not attract attention to your message, then it is worse than useless because your reader will first be attracted to the document and then frustrated that the message can't be found, or will find a message that is at odds with the design. Either way, your reader will be confused and will move to the next step in the persuasion process reluctantly, if at all.

To attract a reader's attention visually to your message, you must know what you want to say, anticipate how your audience might react, and choose the form that will communicate best. The rules presented in Plan Your Design will help make sure you have done this before you start your actual design.

2. Get your reader to understand your message.

2. *The arguments in the message must be understood and comprehended.* Any argument is easier to understand if you can break it down into its components. You probably learned how to apply this method to your writing, beginning with a premise, followed by examples and a conclusion. Good writing uses verbal tools to signal the reader that certain information is a particular step in an argument. Good design uses visual tools to do the same thing. However, visual signals are not "read" or even absorbed consciously; no one ever says, "Ah! A subhead in 14-point Helvetica bold! This must be another point of the conclusion!" Nonetheless, by putting that subhead in 14-point Helvetica bold you make your reader understand that this point *is* part of the conclusion. Several sections of this book will show you how to use visual signals to divide your message into steps and then lead your reader through each step in order.

3. Get your reader to accept your message.

3. *The recipient must learn the arguments contained in the message and come to accept them as true.* Using visual tools to divide your argument, especially a complex argument, into sections makes it easier to learn. You might divide a report into four chapters; each chapter might be further divided into six sections; and each section divided into several parts. Although you can also do this in a typewritten document, the technique is much less effective. Page after page of a typewritten document, no matter how it is divided, will not be as memorable as pages divided with headlines and sub-heads that we can recall by "seeing" them with our mind's eye. And typewriting can't provide the variety of visual clues that good fonts and design can. Subtle spacing, bold, italics, large heads, and subheads can all make meaning clearer and learning easier.

Visual design can even help an argument seem "truer." Because visual signals are absorbed subconsciously, they are very persuasive. A weak point in your conclusion that appears in 14-point Helvetica bold along with all your other points will tend to seem just as strong as the others because it is just as big and bold as they are.

Just the fact that a document is set in type rather than typewritten gives us a visual clue that it is somehow more accurate because we have been conditioned by years of reading books, magazines, and newspapers. Subconsciously we accept that the printed word is more authoritative. By learning how to choose the appropriate fonts and layout for your work, you will learn how to create a visual tone that reinforces your credibility.

4. Get your reader to act on your message.

4. *We act on this learned knowledge and beliefs when there is an incentive to do so.* Visual design cannot, of course, create an incentive that will motivate your reader. But

incentives to action are often more emotional than strictly rational, and visual effects are more evocative than words alone. Although photographs can be strong emotional motivators—by showing the image of an attractive person the reader may identify with, for example—there are many other ways to achieve emotional effects. A particular typeface or arrangement on the page can remind the reader of other publications and trigger a similar emotional response. Advertisers trying to sell products to Apple Macintosh users often mimic Apple's own publication style for just this reason. By understanding how these effects work, you will be able to subtly influence the emotional reaction of your readers.

* Hovland, C. I., Lumsdaine, A. A., & Sheffield, F. D. (1949). *Experiments on mass communication.* Princeton, NJ: Princeton University Press; Hovland, C. I., Janis, I. L., & Kelley, H. H. (1953). *Communication and persuasion.* New Haven, CT: Yale University Press; Hovland, C. I. (1957). *The order of presentation in persuasion.* New Haven, CT: Yale University Press; Hovland, C. I., & Janis, I. L. (1959). *Personality and persuasibility.* New Haven, CT: Yale University Press; Hovland, C. I., & Rosenberg, M. J. (1960). *Attitude organization and change.* New Haven, CT: Yale University Press; Sherif, M., & Hovland, C. I. (1961). *Social judgment.* New Haven, CT: Yale University Press.

How to Use This Book

ALTHOUGH EACH RULE can be read independently, you'll get the most from this book if you read it straight through first. You don't need to study each example diligently—just become acquainted with the general ideas.

Then, the next time you create a document, write it using just the principles you can remember. That way you'll get your ideas down without the distraction of trying to write and design at the same time (although after you become more proficient, that is exactly what you will be able to do). When you are finished with the first draft, use the Document Checklist on page 115 to review your work. Ask yourself whether your document adheres to or violates each rule. If you don't understand the rule, look it up and reread its description.

Whether you're designing a memo, a report, or a newsletter, you'll find that the design principles are the same; however, you'll use (or skip) specific rules depending on the particulars of your document.

By the time you've created a few documents using the ideas in this book, I hope you'll see document design in a new light: not as a mysterious, arty endeavor, but as the very fundamental process of ordering information visually for maximum communication.

LOOKING GOOD ON PAPER

Plan Your Design

WHEN YOU WRITE A REPORT or memo, you naturally look for the best way to express your ideas and consider how it will affect your reader; this is probably so automatic that you take it for granted. But when it comes time to design a document, most people don't plan what they want to say visually and don't consider how their audience will react. Instead, the design just "happens," arising out of personal taste or habit. Yet a document's design, like its text, is a composition; it has its own grammar and syntax, and can communicate meaning just as subtly or powerfully as a carefully worded letter.

To create a document that sells your ideas you have to take the same steps you do when you write: analyze your message to see how it can best be expressed and analyze your audience to anticipate what will create a positive response.

1. Know your message.

Think of your document the way a retailer thinks of a store. A retailer knows she must provide her customers with basic information about the products: what the products are, where they're located on the shelves, how much they cost, and what the store's return policy is. But every retailer knows this alone won't move merchandise. Goods have to be displayed to encourage impulse buying. The strongest selling points have to be clearly listed. And the ambience of the store—the furnishing, decoration, displays, and music—must signal the buyer with emotional cues that tell him he's in the right place for what he wants, whether it's a bargain basement or an exclusive clothing store.

In a business document, your ideas are your merchandise: Your words give the basic information and your visual design both presents that information and creates the atmosphere in which your ideas are sold. Like the store owner, before you put your merchandise on display you must decide what the ambience will be. Begin by imagining the emotional reaction you'd like your reader to have.

For example, let's say you're writing a research report your boss will use to back up a pitch he's making to the president. The ideas you're selling are the data you've found, and the emotional reaction you'd like your boss to feel is one of security in the reliability of your research. What visual cues are associated

Know your message (Fig. a). Just as a store displays merchandise in a setting appropriate to the product, so your words should be displayed in a setting appropriate to your message. Although there is nothing wrong with this layout, it doesn't reinforce the underlying message of this research report, which is that the information inside is accurate and reliable. Instead, the fancy layout makes it look more like an advertisement, which may arouse subconscious doubt about the claims within.

Transportation
Demand
Management
Marketing:

Coordinating Products, Benefits, and Messages

Thomas Seider
Director of Communications
Pacific Data Quest, Inc.
August, 1994

Introduction

For the past 17 years, Pacific Data Quest, Inc. (PDQ) has worked to reduce regular solo commuting by promoting ridesharing and other alternatives: carpooling, vanpooling, telecommuting (working at home, often using a computer and modem), and compressed work weeks (working four ten-hour days a week, for example). These alternatives—known collectively as Transportation Demand Management (TDM)—reduce traffic congestion, air pollution, and the use of energy. Recently, other agencies have begun promoting TDM, each selling TDM in its own way, to address each agency's particular concerns. But the key to any promotion is selling products that address the consumer's concerns, not the promoter's. PDQ has found that the most successful campaigns, in fact, mirror consumer marketing techniques: discovering consumer needs through research, designing products that meet those needs, and communicating product benefits to selected audiences through appropriate communication channels. In the current environment, with a number of campaigns seeking the public's attention, it is likely that the identity of each TDM product and its benefits will be blurred by overlapping, conflicting, and competing messages.

This can be avoided by two means. First, by differentiating and categorizing TDM products so each agency has a clear picture of what is being sold, and second, by coordinating campaigns and messages. This paper seeks to begin this process by reviewing marketing and communication techniques as they apply to TDM products, offering PDQ's experience in the field.

TDM Marketing: Products, Benefits, Communication

Because TDM attempts to change consumer behavior, the marketing theories that best apply are those referred to as social marketing. Putting TDM marketing in terms of social marketing requires the use of some technical terms: target adopter for the individual the campaign wishes to influence; and tangible product base, for a physical object that accompanies a product (such as a transit pass). I use the term "product" for convenience (instead of the more pre-

with solid research? Since most respected research comes from academic institutions, a scholarly paper would provide an excellent model. Following that example, your document should have a single column of double-spaced text, using a traditional font and medium headlines. You would avoid large headlines, too many subheads, bulleted lists, boxes, and other graphic elements. It would probably be a good idea to include some of the information in footnotes, and a bibliography could be included.

If you're designing a resume, the emotional ambience you'd want to create would be entirely different.

This layout, although not as interesting, is better because it communicates a no-nonsense, almost scholarly air.

Transportation Demand Management Marketing: Coordinating Products, Benefits, and Messages

Thomas Seider
Director of Communications
Pacific Data Quest, Inc.
August, 1994

Introduction

For the past 17 years, Pacific Data Quest, Inc. (PDQ) has worked to reduce regular solo commuting by promoting ridesharing and other alternatives: carpooling, vanpooling, telecommuting (working at home, often using a computer and modem), and compressed work weeks (working four ten-hour days a week, for example). These alternatives—known collectively as Transportation Demand Management (TDM)—reduce traffic congestion, air pollution, and the use of energy. Recently, other agencies have begun promoting TDM, each selling TDM in its own way, to address each agency's particular concerns. But the key to any promotion is selling products that address the consumer's concerns, not the promoter's.[1] PDQ has found that the most successful campaigns, in fact, mirror consumer marketing techniques: discovering consumer needs through research, designing products that meet those needs, and communicating product benefits to selected audiences through appropriate communication channels. In the current environment, with a number of campaigns seeking the public's attention, it is likely that the identity of each TDM product and its benefits will be blurred by overlapping, conflicting, and competing mes-

1. Freeburg, Marketing and Market Research (New York: Simpson Press, 1983)

The ideas you're selling are your abilities, expressed in the basic information as your experience. You want your reader to accept that you are competent. But competence is not enough—you want your reader's emotional reaction to be one of enthusiasm and excitement at the idea that you might fill the job. Where might you look for a document model? Consider that in this case *you* are the product—a complicated product with a lot of specifications, but a product nonetheless. And although you might bristle at being compared to a machine, you might look to the advertising used for complicated electronics such as computers. Typically

Know your message (Fig. b). It's important to know the true message of your document—which may be different from the apparent message. For example, in this report to an intrusive supervisor about the writer's job description, the surface message is "here is a description of my duties." However, the true message the writer wants to convey is, "my work consists of more detail than you may want to know." Because this layout is clear and easy to read, it is actually wrong for its purpose.

Position: Director of Public Information

General statement of purpose:

To develop, guide and coordinate company communication via four means: news media (including television, newspapers, magazines and radio), advertising (including multi-media campaigns), publication of sales literature, and direct presentation.

To oversee the three departments responsible for this communication: Public Relations, Advertising, and Sales Publications.

To manage and assist in trade show planning and execution, the company annual meeting, sales events and recognition presentations.

To create new methods of communicating the company messages.

Knowledge and specific skills required for the position.

News media: Knowledge of electronic and print journalism and public relations practices, with emphasis on public awareness procedures for manufacturers and product-oriented story development. *Specific skills include writing, editing, art direction, event planning and interpersonal skills.*

Advertising: Knowledge of advertising theory, with emphasis on advertising for manufacturers, consumer motivation, campaign planning, direct mail and print media, creative development and advertising art production; familiarity with marketing, research, demographic selection and media placement. *Specific skills include concept development, copywriting, photo editing and art direction.*

Publishing: Knowledge of publishing practices, with emphasis on editorial and visual development of sales literature and newsletters, brochures and annual reports; broad knowledge of print production, with emphasis on desktop publishing, typesetting, imagesetting and process color reproduction. *Specific skills including writing, editing, art direction, photo editing, desktop publishing production and design.*

Presentation: Knowledge of graphic design; familiarity with educational techniques. *Specific skills include public speaking, speech writing, art direction and photo editing.*

Other knowledge and skills: managing creative personnel; budgeting, planning.

Internal and external contacts and the purpose of the contacts.

Internal:

Supervises, directly and through subordinates, six positions: Public Relation Manager, Advertising Manager, Creative Director, Art Director, Copywriter and Production Coordinator to guide, coordinate, plan and budget activities.

Directly serves Vice President, Marketing, to communicate company image, position and messages as developed by executive marketing committee.

Directly serves President to write and edit letters, speeches, presentations and opinion-editorials.

---

features are boiled down to the briefest possible descriptions and put in a series of bulleted lists under brief headlines, beginning with the most impressive. Following this example, many resume books advise that a resume start with a summary of experience that lists major accomplishments, not duties tied to a particular job, in a bulleted list. This creates an emotional state of enthusiasm in the reader because the product's desirable qualities are condensed into powerful, short points.

There are even times when you may want your reader's reaction to be boredom. For example, you may

This layout, although not as readable, is actually the better one to use in this case.

Position: Director of Public Information

General statement of purpose: To develop, guide and coordinate company communication via four means: news media (including television, newspapers, magazines and radio), advertising (including multi-media campaigns), publication of sales literature, and direct presentation; to oversee the three departments responsible for this communication: Public Relations, Advertising, and Sales Publications; to manage and assist in trade show planning and execution, the company annual meeting, sales events and recognition presentations; and to create new methods of communicating the company messages.

Knowledge and specific skills required for the position: For news media, knowledge of electronic and print journalism and public relations practices, with emphasis on public awareness procedures for manufacturers and product-oriented story development. Specific skills include writing, editing, art direction, event planning and interpersonal skills. For advertising, knowledge of advertising theory, with emphasis on advertising for manufacturers, consumer motivation, campaign planning, direct mail and print media, creative development and advertising art production; familiarity with marketing, research, demographic selection and media placement. Specific skills include concept development, copywriting, photo editing and art direction. For publishing, knowledge of publishing practices, with emphasis on editorial and visual development of sales literature and newsletters, brochures and annual reports; broad knowledge of print production, with emphasis on desktop publishing, typesetting, imagesetting and process color reproduction. Specific skills including writing, editing, art direction, photo editing, desktop publishing production and design. For presentation, knowledge of graphic design; familiarity with educational techniques. Specific skills include public speaking, speech writing, art direction and photo editing. Other knowledge and skills: managing creative personnel; budgeting, planning.

Internal and external contacts and the purpose of the contacts. Internal: supervises, directly and through subordinates, six positions: Public Relation Manager, Advertising Manager, Creative Director, Art Director, Copywriter and Production Coordinator to guide, coordinate, plan and budget activities. Directly serves Vice President, Marketing, to communicate company image, position and messages as developed by executive marketing committee. Directly serves President to write and edit letters, speeches, presentations and opinion-editorials. Serves managers company-wide to coordinate creative services and advise on written and visual communication. Serves as speaker in company workshops. Works closely with research department to confirm data, measure and assess success of communications.

External: Works with media contacts to facilitate communication through the media. Works with contracted public relations agency to develop messages and review services rendered. Works with vendors and suppliers to secure services and products. Works with other professionals in the public relations community to plan events, share information and offer expertise.

Five major problems that this position is required to solve: For news media, to develop and create news stories and to monitor and exploit news coverage of related events, thereby enhancing public awareness. Specific challenge: to accomplish this in a region already saturated with "created" media interest. For advertising, to find effective ways to promote products to specific audiences, and to measure the effectiveness of these promotions. Specific challenge: to motivate audience to use company products. For publishing, to create and manage publication system and creative services that serve company needs. Specific challenge: to keep pace with expanding and changing demands while delivering high quality and developing new publications and products. For presentations, to create presentations that effectively communicate to critical audiences, most often suppliers and

have a supervisor who is trying to micromanage your department. Let's assume he's asked for a full report on your department's activities for last month and wants you to include all the details. If you think carefully about your message—the idea you're selling—you will understand that it is not to actually make clear how you manage your department. Doing that would invite further meddling from your boss. Your actual message is that you are capable of managing your department yourself. The basic information you present will certainly be what your boss has asked for: the month's activities in detail. Yet the emotional reaction you would like him to have involves his feeling over-whelmed by its complexity and admiring your ability to handle it all—which would make it more likely that he would leave the management of your department to you.

A good model for a complicated, tedious document is a legal contract of some kind—for example, a rental agreement or escrow instructions. The print is small, the lines closely spaced; there are very few headlines and no bulleted lists. Some paragraphs are in all capital letters, and sentences are interrupted midstream with running lists of A., B., C. We also associate great precision and professionalism with legal documents, as well as an esoteric knowledge possessed by highly educated, intelligent people—all qualities that would help you in this case.

When you begin to think about the design of your document, then, look closely at the most fundamental part of your message—not the specific information, but the *reason* you are communicating—and imagine how that message might be expressed in a general style. Don't limit your imagination to business documents; as I have shown, everything from scholarly papers to advertising to escrow instructions can offer you inspiration.

When you are looking for a model to emulate, you don't need to copy the exact font and layout of another publication. You are looking for typical styles that people recognize and which cause the emotional associations: a magazine, a newspaper, a postcard, a wedding invitation, a book, an instructional manual, a warrantee, a textbook, a can of soup—nearly anything with words on it may give you ideas. If you look beneath the surface, you will see how the associations people have with a particular visual presentation might help express your message.

Anticipating the Arrangement Of Information

Once you've decided on the overall style of your document you can move on to plan how you will display the basic information. To some extent, the ambience of your document will help you decide whether your document should be multicolumn (which evokes the emotional response of journalism and advertising) or a single column; whether it will use photos and illustrations or simple diagrams; whether it will be broken up into several small sections with chapters, headlines, subheads, and bulleted lists, or if it will be large blocks of copy. Within the general style you choose, your next task will be to refine it to work for your information. For example, you may have decided that a journalistic approach carries the most positive connotations for your document and so you've decided to use bold headlines and a three-column layout. However, your material divides naturally into three sections, and each of these sections covers five or six topics, each of which could have its own subhead. You could begin the document with one headline, like a magazine article, use subheads for the three sections and then introduce each topic by setting the first sentence of the beginning paragraph in boldface. Another possibility would be to design each of the three sections as its own "article" or chapter, with its own headline, beginning on a new page each time. The topics within each of these sections could then be introduced with subheads.

The specific way you decide to handle divisions such as these will be worked out later in the design process; the point of considering them at this stage is to anticipate how the general arrangement that you choose for your document will affect the organization of the information within it.

2. Know your audience.

Before you commit to an overall style and an emotional ambience for your message, you must consider factors that will affect your audience. Try to answer three questions about your readers: who are they? where are they? and what is their attitude?

Three questions to ask about your readers

1. Who are they? Young or old? Liberal or conservative?

Who is your audience? Your audience may be one person, a small group such as a group of managers, or all potential clients of your business. Try to form a mental picture of your audience—the more specific, the better.

Let's take the case of a single reader—your boss, for example. First, consider what may be so obvious that you overlook it: How good is your boss's vision? Does she have trouble with small type? Make sure you use type that is large enough.

Next, think about the style of your boss. Is she more likely to read *The Wall Street Journal* or *Rolling Stone*? Does he wear a conservative American style suit or an Italian cut? Tastes in publications and clothes offer clues about someone's visual orientation. If your boss is conservative, the extra effort you take to design your document with traditional fonts and justified margins (see Glossary) may add that extra comfort she needs to appreciate your ideas.

Think about your boss's style of cognition. Some people have no trouble grasping concepts in words; others need to visualize. If your boss is harried, switching rapidly from one task to the next, it's more important to break up text into groups of a few paragraphs with subheads to aid in skimming. If your boss is more thoughtful and tends to linger and study long documents, it may be better to develop your argument without the distraction of a lot of subheads. After thinking about it, you may realize that the long memo you planned to write isn't the right way to sell your project. If your boss needs to picture things, perhaps you should put your words into a diagram, similar to a flowchart or GANTT chart.

If you are designing for only one person, you have an ideal situation, because you can carefully study what is effective and what isn't, learning with each document you deliver.

As the size of your audience grows, so does the difficulty of finding a common visual orientation you can appeal to. Look for documents that members of your audience read and respect. For example, a group of managers may all read the president's report and take it as gospel; if so, make your document look like that.

If you are trying to appeal to a very wide range of people—potential clients, for example—look for publications they regularly read, such as trade or professional journals. If you are planning a brochure to sell a product to teenagers, you might adapt a style used for compact disc covers of rock music.

In general, the larger the group you are appealing to, the more conservative should be your design.

Where is your audience? Where someone is greatly affects how they read a document. Let's say you're preparing a report for your boss, and you know that she may present the information from your report at tomorrow's board meeting. Even though your boss may read the report ahead of time in her office, when she goes into the meeting she'll need to present the major points quickly. You can help by beginning the document with an overview—perhaps an introductory paragraph followed by a series of bullet points, one for each major point in the report. You would design the points with space above and below each one so that they'll be easy to see when her eyes are moving from

2. Where are they? What are the physical circumstances under which they'll be reading your message? At a meeting? During a presentation? From a distance?

your report to her audience of board members. Later in the report, you can expand on the bullet points with details, beginning those paragraphs with the exact sentence in boldface, followed by the description.

Now your boss has a document she can use at the place she needs to use it. She can go over all the main points by just looking at the first page. If someone raises a question, she can turn to that page, scanning for the same sentence in boldface. Then she can give the details.

Perhaps you're going to a convention or trade show, and in addition to the usual company literature, you want to create a special flyer advertising a show special. Remember that your readers will be browsing—walking by your table. Their eyes will be skipping over the stacks of literature from several feet away. Your handout better feature a very big headline, or they won't even see it.

A handout that you present to clients during a sales call is different. A big headline would take up space that could be better used for information. Your handout should remind your client of the essential points of your pitch, adding detail. Concentrate on dividing the document into clear sections so that your prospect can find the information he's interested in.

What is your reader's attitude? How much resistance does your reader have to your message? If you're creating a letter that will go out cold to a large mailing list, picture your recipient. He wasn't expecting your letter—it just arrived. There he is, sitting at his desk, opening a stack of mail. The mail he was expecting goes in one pile, junk mail goes in another. Unless your letter can communicate its message fast, it will go in the junk pile. In this case you should create a letter that is a set of brief paragraphs broken up by subheads.

3. What is their attitude? Did they expect your message, or is it a "cold call"? Are they hostile or friendly?

You'll probably want at least two subheads on the first page—more is even better. What your reader will do is skim the subheads to see if there's anything of interest. If there is, he'll begin reading the body of the letter. If you don't include subheads, your reader may skim the first paragraph, and then glance through the rest of the page. He may not see that compelling point you have buried in paragraph three. Don't make him hunt for it—make it a subhead.

There are times when your reader may be in no mood for anything but the most sober design. If your boss is expecting a crucial report, this is not the time to experiment with an unusual font. If you are drafted to write a letter on a delicate matter, don't use subheads! Your letter will look like a sales piece. In this case, there is still design work to be done, although it may be very subtle. For example, think very carefully about where you break your paragraphs. This is a design issue, because the first sentence in a paragraph stands out visually, the last less so, and the middle very little (see Rule 6). This has a psychological effect. If you make a contentious statement at the beginning of a paragraph, it will seem much harsher than if you place it somewhere else. If this is your intent, fine—but think about it.

3. Choose an effective form.

By focusing on your message and envisioning your reader you have studied two parts of the communication process. Next you should consider the carrier of your message—the form of the document.

In evaluating your message, I suggested that you model your document on the style of other publications that carry the emotional tone appropriate for what you want to say. Selecting the form of your doc-

Choose an effective form. The same information will have a different emotional impact depending on the physical form it's presented in. In this example, the announcement of a new telecommuting policy could be presented in any one of these five different ways: as a memo, a letter, a brochure, a flyer, or as an article in the employee newsletter. Each has its own emotional overtones (see text).

ument is a similar exercise, except that here I'm referring to the physical form your document will take. You might, for example, decide that using an advertising style, with several bulleted lists, short paragraphs, and numerous subheads would be best. This style could be used for a memo, a letter, a flyer, or a report. In each case, the form of the document aside from its interior design style has an added emotional impact. Don't assume that the first form you pictured is the best one.

For example, you might start with the assumption that you need a brochure for your new line of services—and you may. But before you decide, consider your options. A business letter is more personal and is easily changed. You can include certain sales points for some recipients, and delete these for others.

Again, imagine the emotional reaction people will have to the form you choose. Let's say you want to get potential clients to attend a product demonstration. You could send a letter, but a formal invitation, with a reply requested, might be better. It connotes a social event, not a sales pitch.

In another case, let's say your boss has asked you to drop a project you think is essential to the company. To convince her, you've decided to produce a report that will explain the facts and persuade her to let you go

ahead. If you hand your boss a full-fledged report with a cover and title page, your boss's first reaction is likely to be, "What are you doing spending all this time on a report about a project I told you to drop?" If you take the same information, edit it tightly, and put it in a long memo, it will seem as if it is something you just dashed off—even if it took days.

Below are a few different kinds of forms and the associations we tend to have with them:

Memos Because memos are exclusive to business, their connotation is strictly one of business, and they carry little personal warmth. Memos are perceived to have been written quickly and delivered quickly, so there is a certain feeling of urgency associated with them. Their information is also thought of as transient, something that will change when new information becomes available.

Letters Letters have more personal warmth than memos or reports. Their information seems more permanent than a memo, less permanent than a report. We think of a letter writer as taking longer to compose a letter than a memo since letters are often longer and go into more detail. Letters have the greatest emotional range of all forms: They're used for everything from very personal communication to junk mail, yet some-how they always retain at least a shadow of the personal touch—which is why direct mail advertising uses them so often.

Handwritten notes Nothing is more personal than a handwritten note, of course, and although it carries none of the other associations—accuracy, reliability, authority—its message of warmth and consideration cannot be replaced by any other form. So powerful is this effect that direct mailers include reproductions of handwritten notes in their mailings fully knowing that recipients realize the note could not possibly be an original.

Reports A report is businesslike, but also has an aura of academia associated with it. It is very impersonal; its overall association is that of objective (and usually dry) information that has taken a good deal of time to compile and which will remain accurate for some time to come. Because reports are multipage documents, a reader will anticipate devoting substantial time to one, even though the report may be no longer than a long letter. The perception is that the information in the report will take longer to absorb. By asking for this time commitment, the report form creates two effects. First, it may intimidate or inhibit some readers who then skim it or don't read it at all. Second, readers who accept the time commitment will devote greater attention to a report than they will to other forms—they are making an investment and they're predisposed to want to see it pay off. In other words, they will be more inclined to accept what they read.

Most annual reports, by the way, can't truly be considered as belonging to the report form; long ago most firms turned them into company advertisements that are more accurately classified as elaborate brochures.

Brochures Because they are sales publications, brochures are overtly trying to persuade, which means that one emotional effect they can have is putting the reader on guard. They contain no personal warmth and are seen as subjective, if not heavily biased. The information they carry may be regarded as accurate or inaccurate, timely or dated—there is nothing in the form itself that makes it seem one way or the other. Since they have multiple pages or panels that are opened one at a time and often reveal strong visuals (either large type, photos, or illustrations), they can create curiosity, anticipation, and a sense of discovery in the reader.

Flyers A flyer is a single sheet of paper, usually letter-sized, advertising something. Like brochures, flyers blatantly try to sell the reader, which creates an initial reservation. The information is subjective, and they are not personal. Unlike brochures, flyers seem more urgent, because they often advertise limited offers.

Catalogs Oddly, the catalog form, which is most obviously a sales piece, has over the past few decades acquired an emotional aura that includes trustworthiness, reliability and even a large amount of personal warmth. These associations probably developed because of mail order firms whose catalogs, like magazines, focused tightly on their customers' interests. A number of these companies raised customer service to new levels; now we regard a well-designed catalog as a sign of the integrity of a company.

Newsletters Before desktop publishing, newsletters were single-column, letter-sized, multipaged publications with simple headlines and no visuals. There were regarded as very timely, and many professionally produced newsletters offered accurate inside information for particular industries, at a premium price. Now newsletters are ubiquitous and are typically three-column, letter-sized, multipaged publications using several headline sizes and replete with illustrations and photos—for all intents, they are mini-newspapers.

The connotation that the earlier style newsletter had was one of vital, fast-breaking, accurate information. For some audiences who remember the old style, this emotional reaction might still be evoked by using the original newsletter form. For most audiences, however, the newer newsletter style has taken over.

Today's newsletter style seeks to create the feeling of objectivity, timeliness, and newsworthiness we associate with newspapers. But because the form has proliferated so rapidly, audiences are becoming jaded to those effects, and tend to react with the same kind of reserve they hold for any advertising. These days, the newsletter form doesn't hold much of its original emotional impact, either from its earlier original form or from the newspaper form it tries to emulate. It's not personal, it's not seen as objective, and, like a brochure, its information can't be regarded as necessarily lasting. The one association it still carries reasonably well is timeliness.

There is one other emotional reaction a reader can get from a newsletter that is worth mentioning. When a person is featured in a newsletter—an employee of the month or a profile of a customer service representative, for example—readers will tend to think of that person as having a moment of fame. They will often have at least a slight bit of elation that somebody they know has appeared in print.

Magazines People have similar emotional reactions to magazines as they do to newspapers: Magazines are generally seen as a source of accurate, objective, timely news. When compared to newspapers, though, information in magazines is regarded as slightly more biased, less up-to-the-minute, but more in-depth. Of the mass-produced published forms, magazines have by far the most personal warmth because most newsstand magazines focus on a very narrow interest of their readers and build a relationship around that activity. (Letters, which would normally be a more personal form, fail to be personal when they're mass produced.) Although the magazine form has been exploited by companies just as the newsletter form has, magazines still carry more of their original impact than do newsletters. A customer who receives a company's magazine will feel less as though she has received an advertisement than if she had received a newsletter, brochure, or form letter.

Books Although it is much rarer for an individual or a business to produce a book as business communication, it has become more common with the advent of desktop publishing. The book form is not just a document that's thicker than a magazine; for the form to have an emotional impact, it must be as similar to a commercially manufactured book as possible, with a cover, a title page, a copyright page and a publisher. It must use good fonts and be well designed.

Because companies have not produced many books as business communications, the form retains almost all of its traditional emotional impact, and among all publications this impact is the most highly regarded. We are taught to revere books from the time we are in grade school. They are seen as authoritative, timely (if recently published), and reliable, and, strangely, a book can be both objective and personal at the same time.

Of course, when you're choosing a form, you won't be able to pick from this entire list; you obviously can't turn a memo into a book. But you probably have more flexibility than you imagine. If you are producing a short document, you could probably choose to make it a memo, letter, or handwritten note. If your company is producing a monthly newsletter with questionable results, you may be able to have a more positive effect on customers by creating a quarterly magazine or semi-annual catalog instead.

Finally, in thinking about form you may come to the conclusion that a printed or written form will not have the emotional effect you need. Instead of writing a letter to a half-dozen clients, you may realize that phoning them would be the best form of communication of all.

4. Aim for a response.

The last step in communication is not simply that your audience gets your message, but that it acts upon that message. Most often the action you want is for your reader to *do* something: you want a client to hire you; you want a customer to buy your merchandise. At other times, you may want your readers to *believe* something: you want the readers of your employee newsletter to believe that your company is a good place to work and that it deserves their ongoing dedication. So in addition to creating a general emotional feeling in your reader (set by the tone of your message and the form of your publication) you must also aim for a specific response from your reader.

Imagine your reader's response in concrete terms—the more vivid and precise, the better. Break that action down into its essential steps. After a reader has seen your piece, what would he do next? Phone your company? Phone a retailer? Drive to a retailer? There is probably a part of your message that answers this question: "Come to the Comedy Express comedy club

Friday night!" or "Call Andy Havens now." Direct mail advertisers call this part of the message the *call to action*. Once you have identified the call to action in your message, you can use design to isolate and emphasize it.

In some business communication, both the call to action and the way your design reinforces it should be subtle. In a business letter that accompanies a resume, for example, you may have easily identified the reaction you want: You want the recipient to hire you. Breaking this down into steps, however, you realize that your reader would never hire you sight unseen. Therefore, the first action step you want your reader to take is to call you. But even this expectation may be unlikely if your potential employer is swamped with applicants. If you were to refine your call to action to "call me at the phone number above," it would very likely be ignored. Looking even more closely, you may be able to see that the first action you want of your reader is simply to remember you. Yet your call to action can hardly be "don't forget about me."

In this case, the call to action must be indirect, and the one that is most often used is this: "I will be calling you in a few days to discuss my qualifications." How can this be a call to action when it doesn't ask the reader to do anything? Yet it does—by telling him to prepare for a call from you. He will not want to answer your call with "Which one were you?" At the very least, he will probably keep your resume handy. The design for this call to action is equally subtle: The sentence should be the first sentence of a short closing paragraph.

The great majority of business communications should contain a call to action. Finding and emphasizing it should be a top priority in your design process. That being said, there are, however, times when your

AdWorld Show Special

AdBudget

Finance Management Software for Advertising Agencies

Compare our features to any other software package! AdBudget has it all. Get AdBudget now for the special AdWorld show price of only $289. You'll get media placement, billing, production cost tracking all handled automatically with AdBudget.

AdBudget

See us at AdWorld Booth 342

communication piece will not contain a call to action. Instead of trying to motivate your readers to act, you will want them to react. It may be handy to think of this as a *call for reaction*. Here I am using this phrase to distinguish between a reader doing something and thinking something.

Most law firms, for example, would not create a brochure with the call to action, "Call our well-respected and competent firm now for help with all your legal needs." Because a law firm's product—legal advice—is entirely quality-dependent (bad legal advice is worthless no matter how cheap), the most important part of

In this layout the suggestion to compare is emphasized by putting the features in a bulleted list. The second (and most important) call to action—to buy the product during the show at the discounted price—is enlarged and put in a more prominent position.

AdWorld Show Special

AdBudget

Finance Management Software for Advertising Agencies

Compare our features to any other software package! You'll get:

- **Media placement**
- **Client billing**
- **Production cost tracking**

all handled automatically with AdBudget. AdBudget has it all.

Get AdBudget NOW for the Special AdWorld Show Price of only

$289

See us at AdWorld Booth 342

---

the message is that the firm is well-respected and competent. This is what I have termed a reaction—a belief the reader should hold. The direct call to action—to retain the firm—can be left as implied. In this case (and in most cases of this kind), the part of your message that aims to create a belief is not just stated; it must be proved. A law firm may list clients or important cases it has handled. The design process for this part of the message would be to bring these points out of the text and highlight them. They might be treated as a list of bulleted items with space between the items, or as a separate box or sidebar.

Sometimes a good, hard search for a call to action or call for reaction will yield neither. This may take you back to reevaluating your message: It's possible that you don't need a printed piece at all. If you find that the action or reaction you want depends a great deal on input from your recipient, consider making a phone call or conducting research to find out more about your audience before you design your document.

5. Put your taste in the background.

Your job is to design in a way that draws attention to the content of your document, not to the design itself. Your judgment is very important in the design. You must decide what to do on the basis of your message, your audience, and the response you want. But your taste should not be a part of your consideration. Aim instead to cater to the taste of your audience.

On simple documents, such as memos, letters, and reports, you can usually anticipate the taste of your audience accurately enough to design your document. On more complicated publications, such as brochures, newsletters, and magazines, you should test your design with an informal survey. When you've created a rough version of a complex publication, show it to a few people, but don't ask them what they think of the design—just watch them. If they begin reading, that's a sign that you've successfully directed their attention to your message. If they say something like "what an interesting font" or "what a clever layout" or "it looks very hip," this could be a sign that your design is overpowering your message. In a consumer publication, this kind of reaction might be an asset; in business, it is usually a drawback, because if a publication's style can create a strong positive reaction in one person it might create a strong negative reaction in another. The only exception to this is if you are trying to appeal to a very style-conscious audience, and in that case it is better to hire a professional designer.

You might think it would be a good idea to show your document to some people in your company's publication department (if it has one), or to a friend who is a designer, but their opinions can mislead you. Although many graphic designers understand the fundamentals of business communications, many more don't. Their interest is often exclusively in graphic style. If you show them a plain, clear, understandable document, they may suggest decoration. You may even like their ideas—it's easy for your personal taste to become engaged at this point, and you will become distracted by what you personally think is interesting or exciting. But there is only one reason you should consider adding any design element to a business document, and that is that you are *certain* it will increase the ease with which a reader can understand your meaning. If it won't—don't.

Once you come up with a good design for one type of document—a report, for example—don't be afraid to repeat it. If it works once to get your message across, it will work again. There is no need to make every document you create look different. You'll get tired of a good design before your readers will, because they see it less often. Make sure a good design has truly outlived its effectiveness before you change it.

Design as You Write

WHETHER YOU REALIZE IT OR NOT, you are making design decisions while you are writing your document. How long you make your paragraphs, which sentences begin and end your paragraphs, whether you put a word in bold, italics, or all capital letters, the number of sections you divide your material into—all of these are, strictly speaking, visual decisions that affect your reader. In this section you will learn to be conscious of these decisions as you write and will learn the standard usage that has evolved in publications.

6. Organize your document into levels.

One of the most powerful functions of design is dividing up complicated ideas into portions. This process interacts with writing. As you write, organize your ideas into levels and sublevels; then show the reader your organization with your design. The most basic level of publication design is deciding where to break your material into paragraphs.

When a reader pages through a document, he will subconsciously note the average length of the paragraphs. Long paragraphs imply that the ideas expressed are more substantial, that each point takes more words to explain, and that the thoughts are denser. Although this adds a feeling of depth, in can also be inhibiting, because it calls for greater concentration and more time to digest. Short paragraphs imply succinct but somewhat shallow ideas, promising a quick read but only a surface examination of a topic. Advertising copy is notorious for short paragraphs—often a single sentence or even a single word—to eliminate any hesitancy on the reader's part and to get a reader quickly through the material. It promises not to bore you with details but instead to give you a quick overview.

Popular publications use paragraphs keyed to their readers. Paragraphs in *The New Yorker*, for example, will often be twice the length of those in *Time*—sometimes three times the length—because *The New Yorker*'s

**Organize your
document into levels.**
Dividing your
information into levels
is similar to creating an
outline, shown here.

Position: Director of Public Information

I. General statement of purpose:

    A. To develop, guide and coordinate company communication via four means: news media (including television, newspapers, magazines and radio), advertising (including multi-media campaigns), publication of sales literature, and direct presentation.

    B. To oversee the three departments responsible for this communication: Public Relations, Advertising, and Sales Publications.

    C. To manage and assist in trade show planning and execution, the company annual meeting, sales events and recognition presentations.

    D. To create new methods of communicating the company messages.

II. Knowledge and specific skills required for the position.

    A. News media:

        1. Knowledge of electronic and print journalism and public relations practices, with emphasis on public awareness procedures for manufacturers and product-oriented story development.

            a. Specific skills include writing, editing, art direction, event planning and inter-personal skills.

    B. Advertising:

        1. Knowledge of advertising theory, with emphasis on advertising for manufacturers, consumer motivation, campaign planning, direct mail and print media, creative development and advertising art production; familiarity with marketing, research, demographic selection and media placement.

            a. Specific skills include concept development, copywriting, photo editing and art direction.

    C. Publishing:

        1. Knowledge of publishing practices, with emphasis on editorial and visual development of sales literature and newsletters, brochures and annual reports; broad knowledge of print production, with emphasis on desktop publishing, typesetting, imagesetting and process color reproduction.

            a. Specific skills including writing, editing, art direction, photo editing, desktop publishing production and design.

    D. Presentation:

        1. Knowledge of graphic design; familiarity with educational techniques.

            a. Specific skills include public speaking, speech writing, art direction and photo editing.

    E. Other knowledge and skills:

        1. Managing creative personnel

readers expect articles of depth. As you write, set your paragraph length to the tone you want to create for your reader: Long paragraphs add substance at the expense of speed; short paragraphs add speed at the expense of substance.

Where you place your sentences in your paragraphs is not only a composition decision but also a design decision. The first sentence of a paragraph is the most prominent. Think of it as a miniheadline, because to a reader who is skimming your document, that's what it

In a publication, the same divisions are created using the visual cues of font size, spacing, bold and medium settings.

Position: Director of Public Information

General statement of purpose:

To develop, guide and coordinate company communication via four means: news media (including television, newspapers, magazines and radio), advertising (including multi-media campaigns), publication of sales literature, and direct presentation.

To oversee the three departments responsible for this communication: Public Relations, Advertising, and Sales Publications.

To manage and assist in trade show planning and execution, the company annual meeting, sales events and recognition presentations.

To create new methods of communicating the company messages.

Knowledge and specific skills required for the position.

News media: Knowledge of electronic and print journalism and public relations practices, with emphasis on public awareness procedures for manufacturers and product-oriented story development. *Specific skills include writing, editing, art direction, event planning and interpersonal skills.*

Advertising: Knowledge of advertising theory, with emphasis on advertising for manufacturers, consumer motivation, campaign planning, direct mail and print media, creative development and advertising art production; familiarity with marketing, research, demographic selection and media placement. *Specific skills include concept development, copywriting, photo editing and art direction.*

Publishing: Knowledge of publishing practices, with emphasis on editorial and visual development of sales literature and newsletters, brochures and annual reports; broad knowledge of print production, with emphasis on desktop publishing, typesetting, imagesetting and process color reproduction. *Specific skills including writing, editing, art direction, photo editing, desktop publishing production and design.*

Presentation: Knowledge of graphic design; familiarity with educational techniques. *Specific skills include public speaking, speech writing, art direction and photo editing.*

Other knowledge and skills: managing creative personnel; budgeting, planning.

Internal and external contacts and the purpose of the contacts.

Internal:

Supervises, directly and through subordinates, six positions: Public Relation Manager, Advertising Manager, Creative Director, Art Director, Copywriter and Production Coordinator to guide, coordinate, plan and budget activities.

Directly serves Vice President, Marketing, to communicate company image, position and messages as developed by executive marketing committee.

Directly serves President to write and edit letters, speeches, presentations and opinion-editorials.

is. He will read the first few words of each paragraph and move on until he has found information that interests him. The next most prominent sentence is the last one of a paragraph, because when a reader is looking for the beginning of a paragraph his eye will often pick up the last few words of the paragraph above it.

Even when a reader does not skim, but reads thoroughly, the first sentence and the last sentence of a paragraph gain emphasis because of where they are placed visually: They begin and end the span of concentration the reader uses to read the paragraph, and these visual cues reinforce the importance of what is said in those sentences.

The next step in dividing your document into levels is to decide where to divide your material into subsections and how many subsections to divide it into. In general, the rule is similar to the one for paragraphs: Short and frequent subsections make the material easier to read but also make it seem less authoritative; long and infrequent subsections do just the opposite.

Additionally, you must decide not only where to divide your material, but how many levels to divide it into. Think of it as exposing the outline beneath the surface of your material. You must decide how much of the outline you want to make visible.

You could, for example, use headlines for your main points, subheads for the points under these, short paragraphs for the points under these, and, finally, bulleted lists for the lowest level of detail. The result would be easy to absorb but too jerky for most documents.

Some people try to make their outline entirely visible by actually writing in outline form. This is a mistake. Except in very rare cases, a document that includes numbered and indented paragraphs is distracting and unnecessary. It's much more efficient to use the traditional tools of publications—headlines, subheads, spacing, boldface type, and bullets—than to use the outline form.

The antithetical approach is to use only a single headline to begin the document and to indicate the divisions by beginning new paragraphs. All subsequent points are expressed in the sentences of each paragraph. For most documents, you will want to fall somewhere in between these extremes, keeping in mind the qualities associated with many or few subsections.

Don't use all uppercase letters, all italics, or all bold for the text of your document. As shown here, these variations are hard to read in a large group. To ensure readability, stick to a font's normal style for the body of your text.

Uppercase BEGINNING IN JUNE, PDQ WILL IMPLEMENT A NEW TELECOMMUTING POLICY WHICH WILL ALLOW EMPLOYEES TO WORK AT HOME BY MEETING CERTAIN MINIMUM REQUIREMENTS. THIS NEW POLICY IS AN EXPANSION OF OUR PILOT TELECOMMUTING PROJECT IN WHICH MANY OF YOU HAVE ALREADY PARTICIPATED.

BEFORE DESCRIBING THE NEW POLICY, I'D LIKE TO REVIEW THE MAJOR FINDINGS OF THE TELECOMMUTING COMMITTEE. FIRST

Italics *Beginning in June, PDQ will implement a new telecommuting policy which will allow employees to work at home by meeting certain minimum requirements. This new policy is an expansion of our pilot telecommuting project in which many of you have already participated.*

Before describing the new policy, I'd like to review the major findings of the Telecommuting Committee.

Bold Beginning in June, PDQ will implement a new telecommuting policy which will allow employees to work at home by meeting certain minimum requirements. This new policy is an expansion of our pilot telecommuting project in which many of you have already participated.

Before describing the new policy, I'd like to review the major findings of the Telecommuting Committee.

Normal Beginning in June, PDQ will implement a new telecommuting policy which will allow employees to work at home by meeting certain minimum requirements. This new policy is an expansion of our pilot telecommuting project in which many of you have already participated.

Before describing the new policy, I'd like to review the major findings of the Telecommuting Committee.

7. Don't use all uppercase letters, all italics, or all bold for the text of your document.

Some people seem to type everything in all capital letters. They may think it adds emphasis to their document, they may not want to have to worry about where to capitalize, they may be computer programmers who are in the habit, or they may just be too lazy to hit the shift key. Whatever the reason, putting a document in all capitals is death to readability.

People don't read letter by letter: They see each

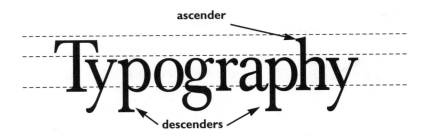

word as a recognizable shape. A big part of a word's shape are the "tops and tails" that lowercase letters have (these are called *ascenders* and *descenders*). Eliminate them, and you are left with boxy shapes that are difficult to read.

Although it's much less common, some people use italics or boldface for the entire text, thinking that it adds style or emphasis. It doesn't. These variations just make your document harder to read. They also eliminate the uses for which italics and bold were created: to add special emphasis.

8. Use italics for emphasis, all capitals for more emphasis, and bold to catch the reader's eye.

Although in headlines you may use italics, all capitals, and bold for different reasons, in text the use of these is traditionally reserved only for special purposes. Occasionally, you may see them used in nonstandard ways in a magazine or annual report—don't let that tempt you away from established uses.

If you want to add emphasis, use italics first:

The project can be completed *if we receive the information by June 1.*

If you really need more emphasis than that, you may use all capitals, but you should realize that using all capitals in a document is the equivalent of shouting:

For the project to be completed, WE MUST RECEIVE THE INFORMATION BY JUNE 1.

Other uses for italics include book titles, plays, and foreign words, as described in journalism and style manuals.

Although you may use boldface for emphasis, it's better to stick to italics and capitals for that job, saving bold for what it does best, which is to **catch the eye.** Boldface stands out like a beacon in text. That makes it perfect for creating reference points between which a reader can skim. You can also use boldface to **highlight names,** if, for example, you're creating an employee newsletter and you want readers to be able to skip to the people they know. Gossip columnists and editors of alumni magazines have used this technique for years.

Use boldface sparingly—too much bold, and nothing will stand out.

9. Express your message with words and images that unite to create meaning.

If your document includes images—illustrations, photographs, or diagrams—think of them not as items to be added at the last minute, but as integral parts of your message, just as your words are.

Images show concrete things best—that which you can see—while words express abstract ideas best—that which you can understand. Use each for its strengths, and avoid duplicating information in both.

Use pictures to show what words can't easily express. In a newsletter story about the signing of a new contract, for example, it isn't necessary to show a picture of two executives actually affixing their signatures. It would be better to use a photo that shows them with expressions that reveal how they feel about the new deal, one that might have been shot before or after they put pens to paper.

Avoid mug shots if you can. Try to use photos that show more than a person's likeness. Show people involved in an activity—working, playing, laughing, or concentrating intensely. Show them in their environment—standing next to the machine they run, sitting by their cluttered desk, walking in the farmland they own, anything that adds information and lets the reader know what kind of person this is. If you must use a mug shot because nothing else is available, make it small. It has limited information to offer.

This layout is better because the word "bugs" has been eliminated and an image has been used to fill in the gap in information. The reader must put together both the words and the image to get the message. Because the reader takes part in creating the message, it becomes more memorable.

> # Most custom software comes with a few little extras.
>
> ### For software without the extras, call Ed Richards
>
> **The Richards Group**
> Custom software for business
> 25 Winston Court • Princeton, NJ 08543
> **(609) 555-1212**

The best photos are those with a natural *hierarchy of attention* within them (see Rule 24)—that is, your eye is led to look at some things first, other things next. Photographers often describe a good shot as having definition between foreground, middle-ground, and background.

Crop out any dead area in the photo, including unnecessary backgrounds such as sky, walls, and desks. (*Cropping* means instructing the printer to print only a portion of the photograph. Don't cut the photo; just mark it so that the unwanted parts are excluded. Use a grease pencil, a crayon-like pencil that makes marks that won't damage the photo and which are easily removed.)Consider cropping very tightly at first, then loosen up if, and only if, this adds important information. Cropping that seems too severe at first often produces the strongest photo. For example, if you are focusing on the emotion on someone's face, try showing only the face—the top of the head, ears, and chin may be irrelevant.

When readers see words and pictures together, they assume there is a relationship between the two. You can exploit this assumption by emphasizing the relationship, and so uniting their messages. A person pictured can come to life, for example, by speaking directly to us as Uncle Sam does when he declares, "I want you!" Imagine in this case how much weaker a non-speaking headline would be; "The army is seeking men and women aged 18 to 34," for example—or if Uncle Sam sat with folded arms.

Other ways to unify words and pictures include making a visual pun or creating an unexpected or incongruous relationship. A question can be posed by a headline and answered by the picture, or a picture can pose a question answered by the headline.

Unity of words and pictures causes the reader to actively participate in the formation of the message, making it more memorable. For example, an advertisement for the local natural gas company had the headline, "Energy Saving Device." All that was pictured was a sweater. By thinking about what the headline has to do with the photo, the reader realizes that the sweater will keep him warm, which means he can turn down his thermostat and save energy. Neither the headline nor the picture would have made any sense by itself. This is the kind of unity that, especially in sales material, is worth striving for.

10. Use only good-quality images.

If you are creating a document and wondering whether to include images when the only ones you have are of poor quality, the answer is, leave them out. High-quality images are common today—color photographs in newspapers and vivid illustrations on computer screens are only two examples that were rare ten years ago. If you use poor-quality images, your audience will make an instantaneous judgment that your document is inferior. And remember that if you do a good job designing the text of your document, using good fonts and a professional layout, a poor-quality image will only look worse by comparison.

This is especially important if you are publishing a brochure, newsletter, magazine, or advertisement that uses photographs. Before a photograph can be printed, its shades of black and gray (called *continuous tone*) must be converted into a pattern of black and white dots of varying size (called a *halftone*). If you look very closely at any printed picture, you can see these dots. Traditionally, this process is called *screening*, because the photograph is rephotographed by a printer through a mesh-like screen, although the same effect can be accomplished now using a scanner. The process is inherently blurry because no sharp lines can be reproduced—only dots, so an out-of-focus photo will become even blurrier, while a washed-out or high-contrast photo will lose detail. High-contrast photos will become even starker because, in general, reproduction increases contrast.

If you are going to reproduce photos in black and white, don't use photos that were originally shot in color, especially if your publication is to be printed by a commercial printer. When a photograph is screened,

Use only good-quality images. If all you have to illustrate your document is a poor-quality image, don't make the mistake of thinking any picture is better than none. Don't use the image—it will only reduce the overall quality of your document. The blurry photo in this flyer adds no important information and detracts from the otherwise good layout.

AdBudget

Finance Management Software for Advertising Agencies

Presents
Advertising Legend

Tom R. Seider

Creator of outstanding campaigns for Kitty Bits cat food, Sleep 'n' Snooze pet beds, and Whif o' Fun catnip.

Hear Tom talk about his style and about how he's used AdBudget on each of his award-winning campaigns.

**Sunday, June 7, 3 p.m.
AdWorld Booth 342**

it is reproduced on printer's process film. Whereas normal black-and-white film records color as appropriate shades of gray, process film records red as black and blue as white. This can play havoc with a color photograph that seems perfectly acceptable. When reproduced, a pinkish glow will become a deep shadow, a blue sky will turn pure white, and ruddy-faced people will turn ghoulish. If you must use a photo originally shot in color, have a professional photo lab convert the color photo into a black-and-white print before you submit it to your printer.

Never try to reproduce a photo clipped from a print-

This flyer is better because it eliminates the photo and uses the space to increase the size of the speaker's name, which is the primary draw anyway.

AdBudget

Finance Management Software for Advertising Agencies

Presents
Advertising Legend

Tom R. Seider

Creator of outstanding campaigns for Kitty Bits cat food, Sleep 'n' Snooze pet beds, and Whif o' Fun catnip.

Hear Tom talk about his style and about how he's used AdBudget on each of his award-winning campaigns.

**Sunday, June 7, 3 p.m.
AdWorld Booth 342**

ed piece. If it has been printed, it has been screened once already, and screening it again may create a *moiré pattern* (a cross-hatch pattern that occurs when one screen pattern interferes with another). It will also lose detail and gain contrast.

When you judge whether you can use a photo, keep in mind the size at which you'll be reproducing it. A good small photo that becomes blurry when you enlarge it to the size you need is no longer a quality image—you must discard it. And a good photo that you must reduce until you can't see what it shows is also no longer a quality image—you can't use it.

Illustrations used to be expensive and difficult to work with in a business document. Now, with computerized clip art, illustrations are easy to include—and that makes them a temptation that should be avoided most of the time. Remember that everything you put in your document should enhance the communication process. Showing an illustration in your sales brochure of a man carrying a briefcase, for example, does nothing to help communicate your message. Because clip art is generic, it is unlikely that any of the images will be directly relevant to your product or service.

In general, avoid humorous clip art images, especially cartoons. Humor is a matter of taste, and too often what you find funny offends your audience.

In business, charts and diagrams are the mainstay of reports. If you include them, make sure they are clear. For example, don't settle for a blurry photocopy of a chart that was produced on a color plotter. See if you can have the chart output on a laser printer. Charts produced by some software and printer combinations (many on mainframe computers and older plotters) print any accompanying words in all-capital, mono-spaced block lettering. You should replace these using a font that is within the family of fonts you've chosen for your document.

Use Fonts Well

COMMUNICATING WITH DESIGN is a matter of attending to many details. When you get the details right, the cumulative effect is a powerful, persuasive, sophisticated document. Because the details seem trivial, most people ignore them and produce poor documents. The details seem trivial because we absorb them subconsciously, and nowhere is this more true than in the proper use of fonts. When used well, their effect is subtle but powerful. When used poorly, their effect is distracting—and powerful.

Technically, a font is the set of characters that make up one size and style of a typeface. For example, all 10-point Helvetica bold characters are one font while 10-point Helvetica italic characters are another. Nowadays, though, most people use the word *font* as a synonym for *typeface,* which is how I will use it here.

Using fonts well requires a lot of effort, but it is worth it. Because fonts carry your words, and words carry your message, their use is the most important part of document design. If you do nothing else in the design of your documents, make sure you use good fonts and arrange your text so that it is highly readable. The guidelines in this will help by giving you a brief but essential education on fonts and their use, which is called *typography.*

11. Pick a classic font.

Most people think the majority of fonts looks alike, so they head straight for the one that looks different. In business, that's like dying your hair purple to stand out. A font is a medium to speak through; it shouldn't speak for itself. A font's style should carry your message, not overpower it. Just as the clothing that's best for business tends to be of classic design, so the fonts you use should also be classics.

How do you know a classic font when you see one? As with wine or racehorses, you need to know its origins. The best fonts have long pedigrees; even new ones are based on styles that have been proved over time and can be classified into families with historical associations. If you know what to look for, you can tell if a font has a noble lineage. Once you become familiar with the emotional tone of the different font families, you can choose from among them to create the feeling you need for the work you're doing.

The differences among classic fonts are subtle, and hard to see at first. The feel of a font is created by

The essential parts of type.

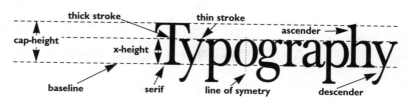

The Five Classic Font Families

Old Style Low contrast between thick and thin strokes; small cap-height and x-height. (Sample: Goudy Old Style.)	 smooth serifs · slanted line of symetry · short descenders · medium ascenders
Transitional Higher contrast between thick and thin strokes; medium cap-height and x-height. (Sample: Baskerville.)	 sharper serifs · slightly slanted line of symetry · medium descenders · medium ascenders
Modern Extreme contrast between thick and thin strokes; medium cap-height and x-height. (Sample: Bodoni.)	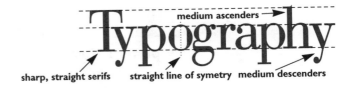 sharp, straight serifs · straight line of symetry · medium descenders · medium ascenders
Slab Serif Low contrast between thick and thin strokes; large cap-height and x-height. (Sample: Clarendon.)	 squared-off serifs · straight line of symetry · short descenders · short ascenders
San Serif No contrast between thick and thin strokes; large cap-height and x-height. (Sample: Helvetica.)	 no serifs · straight line of symetry · short descenders · short ascenders

adjusting small details of the letters' design: the difference between the thick and thin strokes, the angle of the curve in round letters, the finishing stroke of a letter (called a *serif*). Once you become aware of the differences, you can tell what family a font is from and can judge the effect the font will create.

The Five Classic Font Families

Old Style These fonts were designed in the early 1600s to imitate hand-scribed letters drawn with a

Old Style Goudy Old Style	Before describing the new policy, I'd like to review the major findings of the Telecommuting Committee. First, we discovered that productivity actually increased by ten percent, while absenteeism fell by twenty-three percent.
Transitional Baskerville	Before describing the new policy, I'd like to review the major findings of the Telecommuting Committee. First, we discovered that productivity actually increased by ten percent, while absenteeism fell by twenty-three percent.
Modern Bodoni	Before describing the new policy, I'd like to review the major findings of the Telecommuting Committee. First, we discovered that productivity actually increased by ten percent, while absenteeism fell by twenty-three percent.
Slab Serif Clarendon	**Before describing the new policy, I'd like to review the major findings of the Telecommuting Committee. First, we discovered that productivity actually increased by ten percent, while absenteeism fell by twenty-three percent.**
San Serif Helvetica	Before describing the new policy, I'd like to review the major findings of the Telecommuting Committee. First, we discovered that productivity actually increased by ten percent, while absenteeism fell by twenty-three percent.

broad-nibbed pen held at an angle. This family carries the most humanistic and least mechanical feeling. Old Style fonts have only a slight contrast between the thick and thin strokes, and short, irregular curves from the *stem* (the upright stroke of a character) to the *serif* (the finishing stroke of a character). The round characters, such as an <u>O</u> or lowercase <u>e</u>, have a line of symmetry that slants to the left. Some Old Style fonts are Garamond, Goudy Old Style, and Palatino. Use Old Style faces for a warm feel.

Transitional Designed in the mid-1700s, this family is a compromise between the warmth of Old Style and the precision of later fonts. It has features of both. Its tone is humanistic, but with more precision and efficiency. Look for a greater contrast between the thick and thin strokes, long and regular curves from stem to serif, and round characters with a perpendicular line of symmetry. Some transitional typefaces are Baskerville, Bookman, and Times Roman—the most popular font in the English-speaking world. Transitional fonts offer the most neutral emotional tone of all the classic families.

Modern The Industrial Revolution produced Modern fonts, which eliminate all hand-drawn characteristics and instead are rigidly geometrical. Modern fonts have extreme contrast between thick and thin strokes, sharp angles where the stem meets the serif, and round characters with a perpendicular line of symmetry. Examples include Didot and Bodoni. The impression they convey is one of calculation. Modern fonts feel efficient, machinelike, and cold.

Square Serif From the late 1800s, fonts in this family feel mechanical, but not as extreme as the Moderns. They have little or no contrast between thick and thin strokes, short curves (or sometimes only angles) from stem to serif, and round characters with a perpendicular line of symmetry. Their most distinctive feature is thick, squared-off serifs, which are sometimes as thick as the main stroke itself. Examples of Square Serif fonts are Egyptian, Century Schoolbook, and Lubalin Graph. The mood they convey is refined precision.

Sans Serif During the early 1900s, decoration was stripped from everything—including fonts. The result in type design were the Sans Serif ("without serifs") fonts. These fonts have no contrast at all between any of the strokes: the letters appear to be made up of uniform lines (although there are often very slight adjustments). Examples include Helvetica, Univers, and Avant Garde. The feeling is no-nonsense functionalism—crisp in short paragraphs, but a little stern for long text blocks.

Before you pick a font, see if it seems to be a member of one of the five families. If it seems unlikely to be from one of these families, avoid it. Type that falls outside the classic families will draw attention to itself rather than to the ideas you're trying to express.

In business, the best all-around family is Transitional, followed by Sans Serif and Square Serif. Use Old Style fonts if you need to add warmth, and use a Modern font only if you are certain you need that much severity, and only if you know what you're doing: Modern fonts are hard to read in text unless they're well spaced (see Rule 18).

The popularity of these families changes with the times. In the 1940s and 1950s, for example, companies were proud to be machinelike and crisp. Modern and Square Serif typefaces were everywhere: IBM, for example, used Bodoni text in its publications and advertisements throughout the 1950s, and its familiar IBM logo was created with Square Serif letters. The 1960s and 1970s brought revolt against conformity and an emphasis on a humanistic outlook. People went back to nature and back to handmade crafts; designers went back to Old Style fonts.

While the popularity of these families change, their connotations don't. Don't try to follow the trends—just choose from a family that sets the right tone for your job.

Although it's easiest to pick one font for your whole document, you can combine fonts and so combine

Choose a legible font.
The legibility of even the classic fonts is not the same. This page of Helvetica is not difficult to read, but is not as easy as the page of Century Schoolbook shown on the opposite page.

Position: Director of Public Information

General statement of purpose: To develop, guide and coordinate company communication via four means: news media (including television, newspapers, magazines and radio), advertising (including multi-media campaigns), publication of sales literature, and direct presentation; to oversee the three departments responsible for this communication: Public Relations, Advertising, and Sales Publications; to manage and assist in trade show planning and execution, the company annual meeting, sales events and recognition presentations; and to create new methods of communicating the company messages.

Knowledge and specific skills required for the position: For news media, knowledge of electronic and print journalism and public relations practices, with emphasis on public awareness procedures for manufacturers and product-oriented story development. Specific skills include writing, editing, art direction, event planning and interpersonal skills. For advertising, knowledge of advertising theory, with emphasis on advertising for manufacturers, consumer motivation, campaign planning, direct mail and print media, creative development and advertising art production; familiarity with marketing, research, demographic selection and media placement. Specific skills include concept development, copywriting, photo editing and art direction. For pub-

---

tones. (For some guidance on how to mix fonts, see Rule 13.) Typically, you may want to choose a headline font that provides a sharp contrast to the body text font. One common combination is to choose a Sans Serif font such as Helvetica as your headline font for its precision, and then to soften that effect (as well as increase readability) by using a Transitional font such as Times Roman for the text.

Don't let the names of fonts throw you—if you see fonts that look the same but have different names, you're not going crazy. Many fonts that are for all practical purposes identical have been given different

Because of its large,
open characters and
strong serifs, Century
Schoolbook is a very
legible font.

Position: Director of Public Information

General statement of purpose: To develop, guide and coordinate company communication via four means: news media (including television, newspapers, magazines and radio), advertising (including multi-media campaigns), publication of sales literature, and direct presentation; to oversee the three departments responsible for this communication: Public Relations, Advertising, and Sales Publications; to manage and assist in trade show planning and execution, the company annual meeting, sales events and recognition presentations; and to create new methods of communicating the company messages.

Knowledge and specific skills required for the position: For news media, knowledge of electronic and print journalism and public relations practices, with emphasis on public awareness procedures for manufacturers and product-oriented story development. Specific skills include writing, editing, art direction, event planning and interpersonal skills. For advertising, knowledge of advertising theory, with emphasis on advertising for manufacturers, consumer motivation, campaign planning, direct mail and print media, creative development and advertising art production; familiarity with marketing, research, demographic selection and media placement. Specific

names by their suppliers. So, for example, Helios, Sans, and Swiss are all alternative names for Helvetica.

12. Choose a legible font.

There's a difference in the readability of even the best fonts. Make sure the font you've chosen is going to be legible in the circumstances in which you're going to use it. In general, Modern and Sans Serif fonts are harder to read than others.

Fonts with serifs are easier to read because serifs help define the shapes of the letters and help the reader's eye flow in a horizontal direction. They also provide a better fit between the letters, so that they form distinctive word-shapes instead of groups of isolated letters. Sans Serif fonts lack these features and often have confusingly similar characters, notably the capital *I*, lower case *l*, and numeral *1*. For example, in Helvetica, the word "Ill" looks like this: Ill.

Modern fonts can be hard to read because at sizes appropriate for text the thick vertical strokes overpower the thin horizontal strokes. This makes it harder to see the word-shapes that are essential to readability.

If you use either of these families, make sure you have room to use them in a larger size—11 point is a minimum; 12 point is even better. If you can control the space between lines with your particular word processor or desktop publishing program, add some space (see Rule 18).

Another factor influencing a font's readability is its *x-height*. This is the height of the lowercase letters compared to the overall font size. The term *x-height* is taken from the size of a lowercase *x*, which defines this height. All other things being equal, a font with a large x-height will look bigger and will be more readable than a font of the same size with a small x-height. Although a small x-height is generally a characteristic of older fonts, many of these have been redesigned with larger x-heights.

Fonts with small x-heights will have longer ascenders and descenders, often giving them a graceful appearance. Because there is more space above and below the lowercase letters, these fonts need little, if any, added space between lines. Fonts with large x-heights, on the other hand, appear larger and need more line space to keep them readable.

When you fill a page with type it has what designers call *color*, that is, it appears as a darker or lighter shade of gray. Some fonts look dense and can be forbidding. To judge this quality, you must see a sample set en masse, with the size and line spacing you intend to use. If you'll be breaking up your text with several subheads, then a dense font isn't so bad; otherwise, stick with lighter fonts.

13. Don't use several different fonts in one document.

Each font has a unique voice. Using too many is like having too many people talking at the same time—the result is confusion.

If, in the same section of your document, you mix fonts from a number of families, choosing, for example, Garamond (Old Style), Baskerville (Transitional), Bodoni (Modern), and Helvetica (Sans Serif), the feelings communicated by them will fight each other. Choosing a number of fonts from the same family doesn't work either. You might suppose, for example, that Garamond, Caslon, and Palatino—all from the Old Style family—would complement each other. Instead, they look as if they should match, but don't.

As a rule of thumb, don't mix more than three different fonts in one visual presentation. To create variety, use variations of the same font (bold, extra bold, italic, all capitals, and so forth), and different sizes. If you do use different fonts, assign them to different levels of your document. For example, you could use Bodoni for the headlines, Helvetica for the subheads, and Baskerville for the text. Each font will then speak in a clear voice at its own level.

Fonts that are similar in style should be separated by size; otherwise the fonts will look as if they should match, but don't. For example, you could safely use Baskerville for headlines and the similar-looking Times Roman for text, but it would be risky to use Times

AdWorld Show Special

AdBudget

Finance Management Software for Advertising Agencies

Compare our features to any other
software package! You'll get:

- **Media placement**
- o Client billing
- **Production cost tracking**

all handled automatically with
AdBudget. AdBudget has it all.

Get AdBudget NOW for the Special AdWorld Show Price of only

$289

See us at AdWorld Booth 342

Roman for subheads in this case because they would be too close in size to the Baskerville headlines and would invite comparison. The two would look mismatched.

The more dissimilar the fonts are, the closer in size they can be. One good use is to run in a subhead as the first few words of a paragraph, but in a very different font. Here, Helvetica bold serves as a lead-in subhead to a paragraph set in Times Roman:

Eighteen years of experience Our company's customer service via phone has grown

This layout uses only three different fonts, but at different sizes and weights, to achieve variety.

from a single phone line in 1974 to six toll-free numbers. The teleservices department has eighteen years of experience answering the public's calls and working on computer terminals to fulfill their needs.

You can use this technique with the subhead in bold of the same font you're using for text, but using a different font is even more effective. Note that when the difference between the two fonts is clear, there is no need for a period after the lead-in subhead to separate it from the text.

14. Set your font size and margins so that between thirty and ninety characters fit on each line.

Set your font size and margins so that between thirty and ninety characters fit on each line.
Too many or too few words on each line create readability problems, as shown below.

After you've set the margins and the size of your font, find the number of characters in an average line by adding up all the characters in five lines and then dividing by five (remember that each space counts as a character). If you've got more than ninety characters, that's too many: Your reader might find himself "double reading" a line because it's so far back to the beginning. If you've got fewer than thirty, that's too few: Your reader will be driven crazy by the frantic back-and-forth eye movement it takes to read your document. If you're creating more than one column, check the character count of one column (not of the combined columns) to make sure it's within these guidelines. If not, change either your type size or margins.

Position: Director of Public Information

General statement of purpose: To develop, guide and coordinate company communication via four means: news media (including television, newspapers, magazines and radio), advertising (including multi-media campaigns), publication of sales literature, and direct presentation; to oversee the three departments responsible for this communication: Public Relations, Advertising, and Sales Publications; to manage and assist in trade show planning and execution, the company annual meeting, sales events and recognition presentations; and to create new methods of communicating the company messages.

Too many words causes the reader to re-read lines.

Position: Director of Public Information

General statement of purpose: To develop, guide and coordinate company communication via four means: news media (including television, newspapers, magazines and radio), advertising (including multi-media campaigns), publication of sales literature, and direct presentation; to oversee the three departments responsible for this communication: Public Relations, Advertising, and Sales Publications; to manage and assist in trade show planning and execution, the company annual meeting, sales events and recognition presentations; and to create new methods of communicating the company messages.

Knowledge and specific skills required for the position: For news media, knowledge of electronic and print journalism and public relations practices, with emphasis on public awareness procedures for manufacturers and product-oriented story development. Specific skills include writing, editing, art direction, event planning and interpersonal skills. For advertising, knowledge of advertising theory, with emphasis on advertising for manufacturers, consumer motivation. campaign planning, direct mail and print media, creative development and advertising art production; familiarity with marketing, research, demographic selection and media placement. Specific skills include concept development, copywriting, photo editing and art direction. For publishing, knowledge of publishing practices, with emphasis on editorial and visual development of sales literature and newsletters, brochures and annual reports; broad knowledge of print produc-

Too few words causes uncomfortable back-and-forth eye movement.

Position: Director of Public Information

General statement of purpose: To develop, guide and coordinate company communication via four means: news media (including television, newspapers, magazines and radio), advertising (including multi-media campaigns), publication of sales literature, and direct presentation; to oversee the three departments responsible for this communication: Public Relations, Advertising, and Sales Publications; to manage and assist in trade show planning and execution, the company annual meeting, sales events and recognition presentations; and to create new methods of communicating the company messages.

Knowledge and specific skills required for the position: For news media, knowledge of electronic and print journalism and public relations practices, with emphasis on public awareness procedures for manufacturers and product-oriented story development. Specific skills include writing, editing, art direction, event planning and interpersonal skills. For advertising, knowledge of advertising theory, with emphasis on advertising for manufacturers, consumer motivation. campaign planning, direct mail and print media, creative development and advertising art production; familiarity with marketing, research, demographic selection and media placement. Specific skills include concept development, copywriting, photo editing and art direction.

The recommended number of words provides for comfortable reading.

15. Double-check the size of your font.

As you may know, fonts are measured in something called *points*. A point is approximately 1/72 of an inch. Twelve points make a pica, which is a standard measurement used in graphic design. For example, picas are used to measure the width of a column; an 18-pica column is about three inches wide.

What many people don't realize is that all 12-point type is not the same size. For example, 12-point Helvetica is bigger than 12-point Garamond. Why? Because the point size is not a measure of the height of the letters, but of a part of the font that no longer exists.

The point system evolved when all fonts were cast in metal. The part of each piece of type that was pressed against the paper to create the printed image was cast onto a nonprinting block called the *body*. The point size of a font referred to the size of the font's body, not the size of the printed characters. Some fonts were designed to be "large on the body" and some "small on the body," so although two styles might both have been cast on a 12-point body, the difference in printed size was considerable.

Even though computerized fonts have no body to measure, the system persists. The result is that at a given point size some styles will be much smaller than others and will have extra space between the lines (even if you don't add any), while other styles will look large and tightly spaced.

Another difference between fonts of the same point size is that some are much wider than others. For example, 12-point Bookman will take up much more room than 12-point Times Roman. Even the same font may vary in size between two different suppliers, 12-point Helvetica from one company being larger than 12-point Helvetica from another, for example.

Double-check the size of your font. The actual size of a font varies considerably depending on the style. This text is in 10-point Goudy Old Style. On the opposite page, the same amount of text has be set in10-point Clarendon.

General statement of purpose: To develop, guide and coordinate company communication via four means: news media (including television, newspapers, magazines and radio), advertising (including multi-media campaigns), publication of sales literature, and direct presentation; to oversee the three departments responsible for this communication: Public Relations, Advertising, and Sales Publications; to manage and assist in trade show planning and execution, the company annual meeting, sales events and recognition presentations; and to create new methods of communicating the company messages.

Knowledge and specific skills required for the position: For news media, knowledge of electronic and print journalism and public relations practices, with emphasis on public awareness procedures for manufacturers and product-oriented story development. Specific skills include writing, editing, art direction, event planning and interpersonal skills. For advertising, knowledge of advertising theory, with emphasis on advertising for manufacturers, consumer motivation, campaign planning, direct mail and print media, creative development and advertising art production; familiarity with marketing, research, demographic selection and media

These differences mean that you can't just assume that if you use a 12-point font it will be the right size for your job. One 12-point font can be as much as 20 percent larger than another—and make your document 20 percent longer.

Before you decide to use a particular font at a particular size for your entire document, print out a few paragraphs in several different fonts as samples. Experiment with different amounts of line spacing and different sizes. Only by comparing the actual documents can you really judge the readability of a font at the size you intend to use it.

Although the point size is the same, Clarendon is actually much bigger, and would add several pages to a long document.

General statement of purpose: To develop, guide and coordinate company communication via four means: news media (including television, newspapers, magazines and radio), advertising (including multi-media campaigns), publication of sales literature, and direct presentation; to oversee the three departments responsible for this communication: Public Relations, Advertising, and Sales Publications; to manage and assist in trade show planning and execution, the company annual meeting, sales events and recognition presentations; and to create new methods of communicating the company messages.

Knowledge and specific skills required for the position: For news media, knowledge of electronic and print journalism and public relations practices, with emphasis on public awareness procedures for manufacturers and product-oriented story development. Specific skills include writing, editing, art direction, event planning and interpersonal skills. For advertising, knowledge of advertising theory, with emphasis on advertising for manufacturers, consumer motivation, campaign planning, direct mail and print media, creative development and advertising art production; familiarity with marketing, research, demographic selection and media

16. Set your text flush left or justified.

With most word processors and desktop publishing programs, you can align text in one of four different ways: *flush left, centered, flush right,* or *justified.* (Flush left is sometimes called *left-justified* or *rag right;* flush right is sometimes called *right-justified* or *rag left;* justified is sometimes called *flush left and right.*) For the text of your document you should most often choose flush left.

Flush left text is the most readable style of alignment for two reasons. First, it provides a consistent place for

Set your text flush-left or justified. Shown here are the four basic ways of setting text. Flush left and justified are easiest to read because they provide a consistent place for the reader's eye to return to at the beginning of each line.

Flush left (also called rag right) General statement of purpose: To develop, guide and coordinate company communication via four means: news media (including television, newspapers, magazines and radio), advertising (including multi-media campaigns), publication of sales literature, and direct presentation.

Justified (also called flush left and right) General statement of purpose: To develop, guide and coordinate company communication via four means: news media (including television, newspapers, magazines and radio), advertising (including multi-media campaigns), publication of sales literature, and direct presentation.

Flush right (also called rag left) General statement of purpose: To develop, guide and coordinate company communication via four means: news media (including television, newspapers, magazines and radio), advertising (including multi-media campaigns), publication of sales literature, and direct presentation.

Centered General statement of purpose: To develop, guide and coordinate company communication via four means: news media (including television, newspapers, magazines and radio), advertising (including multi-media campaigns), publication of sales literature, and direct presentation.

---

the reader's eye to return to after reading each line. Second, it provides equal space between each word, which delivers the flow of information in a steady reading rhythm.

Justified alignment is the next most readable. It too has an even left margin. But to create the even right margin, space between the words must be uneven. In some cases, justified alignment even causes the computer to put extra space between the letters of a word. In extreme cases, where the width of the column is too narrow, one word may be spaced out to occupy an entire line. This spacing between words or letters can, depending on its severity, reduce readability by disturbing the reading rhythm. These problems are usually solved by increasing the number of characters per line, which then makes justified text very readable.

Both flush right and centered alignments are much less readable than flush left or justified because of the uneven left margins. Reading long blocks of this alignment is very tiring.

Aside from readability, there are other reasons to choose one setting over another, and this has to do with the connotations that alignment has. Justified and centered alignment, because of their symmetry, are the most formal styles. While centered alignment should never be used for long blocks of text, it is appropriate for headlines, subheads, or short lines of text, such as an invitation or advertisement.

You can use justified alignment for text if you want to achieve a bookish, formal appearance, but take extra care that your document's line length is long enough (see Rules 14 and 17). Never justify headings or subheads: The added space is far too noticeable and, frankly, ugly.

Flush left alignment is only slightly less formal than justified and is appropriate for blocks of text in the great majority of situations. Headings that are flush left are slightly less formal than centered, but they communicate more quickly because they begin at the left margin. Either centered or flush left headings can be used with flush left text.

The connotation of flush right alignment can be summed up as "untraditional" and should be used appropriately. As noted, text blocks should never be aligned flush right—it is too hard to read. A flush right heading can be used appropriately in two situations: first, on a page by itself or isolated from surrounding text—on the front of a brochure, for example, or in the top panel of an advertisement; second, when the heading "butts up" against a box (a photo or graph, for example), a margin, or a block of text. Flush right alignment should not be used as a standard heading above text blocks.

Captions can sometimes be set flush right when they butt up against the photo they describe; this is one of the better uses of flush right alignment. In most other cases, avoid flush right alignment; it is hard to use well, and its untraditional connotation makes it inappropriate for most business uses.

17. Don't justify narrow columns.

Although Rule 16 explains why justified alignment should not be used on narrow columns, this idea is important enough (and violated often enough) to require its own rule.

If a narrow column is justified, the spaces between words will be too large, because there is less type to work with. This creates *rivers*—white space between words that creates a vertical channel that runs up and down the column, making the text hard to read.

How can you tell if a column is too narrow? Rule 14 suggests margins that allow between thirty and ninety characters to fit on each line. For justified alignment, allow at least forty characters per line; longer is even better.

18. Add space between lines of hard-to-read type.

The amount of space between lines of type is traditionally called *leading* (pronounced like the metal, because originally strips of lead were used to separate lines of type); today it is also called *line spacing*. Line space is measured in points, and is measured from one *baseline* to the next (the baseline is the imaginary line

Don't justify narrow columns. The column on the left is set justified, causing too much space between words. The column on the right, which is set flush left, is better.

General statement of purpose: To develop, guide and coordinate company communication via four means: news media (including television, newspapers, magazines and radio), advertising (including multi-media campaigns), publication of sales literature, and direct presentation; to oversee the three departments responsible for this communication: Public Relations, Advertising, and Sales Publications; to manage and assist in trade show planning and execution, the company annual meeting, sales events and recognition presentations; and to create new methods of communicating the company messages.

Knowledge and specific skills required for the position: For news media, knowledge of electronic and print journalism and public relations practices.

General statement of purpose: To develop, guide and coordinate company communication via four means: news media (including television, newspapers, magazines and radio), advertising (including multi-media campaigns), publication of sales literature, and direct presentation; to oversee the three departments responsible for this communication: Public Relations, Advertising, and Sales Publications; to manage and assist in trade show planning and execution, the company annual meeting, sales events and recognition presentations; and to create new methods of communicating the company messages.

Knowledge and specific skills required for the position: For news media, knowledge of electronic and print journalism and public relations practices.

on which the lowercase characters sit, and below which the descenders hang). If two points of line space are added to a 10-point font, this is called "10 on 12" or "10 leaded two points" and is written 10/12. A 10-point font set without extra line space is called "10 on 10" or "10 set solid" and is written 10/10.

Adding line space increases readability in two ways. First, it separates the lines, making it easier to find the beginning of each new line. Second, it adds space above and below the type, making the shapes of the words easier to recognize.

Although it's acceptable for a line of type to have up

Add space between lines of hard-to-read type. Helvetica is less legible than other typefaces, and so needs space between the lines. This example is set with too little line space.

General statement of purpose: To develop, guide and coordinate company communication via four means: news media (including television, newspapers, magazines, and radio), advertising (including multi-media campaigns), publication of sales literature, and direct presentation; to oversee the three departments responsible for this communication: Public Relations, Advertising, and Sales Publications; to manage and assist in trade show planning and execution, the company annual meeting, sales events, and recognition presentations; and to create new methods of communicating the company messages.

  Knowledge and specific skills required for the position: For news media, knowledge of electronic and print journalism and public relations practices, with emphasis on public awareness procedures for manufacturers and product-oriented story development. Specific skills include writing, editing, art direction, event planning and interpersonal skills. For advertising, knowledge of advertising theory, with emphasis on advertising for manufacturers, consumer motivation, campaign planning, direct mail and print media, creative development and advertising art production; familiarity with marketing, research, demographic selection and media

to ninety characters in it (see Rule 14), the longer a line gets, the harder it is to read. If your line contains more than sixty characters, add space between the lines to make them more readable. The amount to add depends on the font (some need less than others—see Rule 15), but it should be at least two points.

Some fonts are inherently more difficult to read than others (notably, those of the Sans Serif and Modern families—see Rule 12) and can be made more readable by adding line space. Fonts that are large on the body (in other words, large for their point size) also need extra line space.

Added line space in this example makes the text easier to read.

General statement of purpose: To develop, guide and coordinate company communication via four means: news media (including television, newspapers, magazines, and radio), advertising (including multi-media campaigns), publication of sales literature, and direct presentation; to oversee the three departments responsible for this communication: Public Relations, Advertising, and Sales Publications; to manage and assist in trade show planning and execution, the company annual meeting, sales events, and recognition presentations; and to create new methods of communicating the company messages.

Knowledge and specific skills required for the position: For news media, knowledge of electronic and print journalism and public relations practices, with emphasis on public awareness procedures for manufacturers and product-oriented story development. Specific skills include writing, editing, art direction, event planning and interpersonal skills. For advertising, knowledge of advertising theory, with emphasis on advertising for manufacturers, consumer motivation, campaign planning, direct mail and print media, creative development and advertising art production; familiarity with marketing, research, demographic selection and media

19. Reduce the letterspace, word space, and line space when you use larger fonts.

All word processing programs and desktop publishing programs automatically control the space between letters (*letterspace*), between words (*word space*), and between lines (*line space*). For most documents, you don't need to adjust these values. Memos, letters, and most reports look fine using the automatic spacing determined by your software. But when you begin to design more sophisticated documents, such as newsletters, magazines, and advertisements, the fine adjustments you make to these spacing values will mean the difference between a publication that looks professional and one that doesn't. Although all desktop publishing programs and the major word processing programs support adjustable letterspacing, word spacing, and line spacing, some older word processing programs do not. Letterspace and word space are usually measured as a fraction (often tenths or hundredths) of an *Em-space*, which is the width of the uppercase letter M̲ in the font you're using. An *En-space*—the width of the uppercase letter N̲—is another common measure. Line space is usually measured in points.

Adjusting these values is necessary at larger point sizes because as a font's size increases, an optical illusion occurs: The white space around the type seems to grow disproportionately larger. For example, a 10-point font set on automatic spacing will look fine, but a 48-point font will look too loose—the individual letters will stand alone rather than form words, the words will seem far from each other, and the lines of type will look isolated. The larger the type, the more all these spaces must be tightened up. Let's consider letterspacing first.

There are two ways to reduce letterspacing: overall letterspacing and *kerning*. Overall letterspacing adjustment brings all the letters closer together, while kerning means precisely fitting two letters together—often called a *kerning pair*. Different word processors refer to overall letterspacing with different terms. Microsoft Word, for example, calls it "condensed spacing." Other word processors may refer to any adjustment of the space between letters as kerning.

As a rule of thumb, consider reducing the overall letterspacing of any font size larger than 24 points, and definitely reduce the letterspacing if you're using headlines of 48 points or larger. Different fonts require more or less tightening depending on the font's design. Your goal should be to tighten letters as close as they can be without touching.

You'll notice that when you tighten the overall letterspacing, some letter combinations will be tight enough and others will still have gaps between them owing to the shape of the individual letters. This is where kerning comes in. In many word processing programs the adjustment is made the same way as tightening the overall letterspacing, except that you select only the two letters you are adjusting and set a value just for that pair.

Needless to say, good kerning can take a lot of time, and you must consider how important it is to your document to get all the letterspacing just right. If you are designing a report with several chapters, each of which will have a 30-point headline, it's probably not worth kerning them—tightening up the overall spacing should improve them enough. But if you're designing a brochure with a single 72-point headline on the cover, you should go to the extra effort to make sure the letterspacing and kerning look good.

Once you have tightened the space between letters, check to see if the space between words is also too large. The word space will have been reduced when you reduced the overall letterspacing, but it may not have been enough. At smaller sizes, the space between words set automatically by your software is about the width of the lowercase letter n̲. At font sizes above 24 points, this begins to look too large. While the amount to reduce depends on the size of the font and its design, keep in mind that it would not be unusual to reduce the word space in a 72-point headline to the width of the lowercase letter i̲. Although that may seem like a very small amount of space, at that size it is plenty for your reader to distinguish where one word ends

Reduce the letterspace, word space, and line space when you use larger fonts. (Fig. a). Here is an example of a 36-point Baskerville headline before letterspace, word space, and line space reduction. The next three illustrations show the results of removing the extra space.

Do You Want Average AVR Ratings or MegaRatings?

and the next one begins, and that's all your reader needs.

To adjust the word space independently from the overall letterspace, you may, on some word processors, need to adjust the value for each word space separately, just as you did when you kerned some letters. And as with kerning, this kind of attention to detail is needed only for brief headlines that will receive a lot of attention, as in an advertisement.

When you allow your word processor to automatically determine the space between the lines of type—the line space—it calculates this value as a percentage

(Fig. b). Here the overall letterspace (which includes the space between words) has been reduced. Notice that in some places the letters are still too far apart and in others they are too close.

Do You Want Average AVR Ratings or MegaRatings?

of the size of the font; typically, about 120 percent. So if you're using a 10-point font on the automatic setting, your font is 10-point font on 12 points of line space. When you set headlines, your software uses the same percentage, so that a 60-point font will be set on 72 points of line space, which is way too much.

In general, most headlines over 24 points look better if you use the font's size as its line spacing value, so a 60-point headline would be set on 60 points of line space. Some fonts—ones that are small for their point size—will look best in larger sizes if the line spacing is actually *less* than the font's point size—a 60-point head-

(Fig. c). In this
example, the headline
has now been kerned.
In some places,
letterspace has been
reduced (between the Y
and the o in "You," for
example). In other
places, letterspace has
been added where the
letters were too tight
(between the *t* and *i* in
"Ratings"). Finally, the
word space was
reduced between all the
words.

Do You Want Average AVR Ratings or MegaRatings?

line set on 56 points of leading, for example, so that the
descenders fall into the next line of type. Or it may be
necessary if your headline consists of all capital letters,
because there are no descenders to fill the space below
the baseline.

Another spacing problem that occurs in type set in
larger point sizes is that the space between the lines
may look unequal even when it is exactly the same
when measured from baseline to baseline. This happens when the words in one line have no ascenders or
decscenders, making it look as if they have extra space
above or below them, respectively. To fix this, adjust

(Fig. d). The last step is to reduce the line space. The line space has been reduced from about 43 points (the automatic setting) to 32 points (even though the font size is still 36-point). Notice how the lower-case *g* in the word "Ratings" fits into the space between the *R* and the *t* of the next line. This kind of close fitting is common in advertising.

Do You Want Average AVR Ratings or MegaRatings?

the line space visually, and don't worry that the spacing is actually different from line to line.

This kind of fine adjustment isn't necessary for a publication that uses a lot of headlines—a newsletter, for example. It's usually only needed if you have one large headline that serves as a strong graphic element on an advertisement, poster, or brochure.

Because of the difference between font designs, sizes, and the actual words you're using, there is no standard to determine how much space you should put between lines of large type. The only way to achieve a good look is by experimenting and seeing what looks best.

20. Use typographical characters.

In typesetting (as opposed to typewriting), letters, apostrophes, quotation marks, numerals, and inch and foot marks are unique. You should not use, for example, the capital letter O for a zero—it won't look right, and it won't line up correctly if you use it in columns of numbers.

With the advent of desktop publishing and word processing, this is one of the most abused rules of traditional typography. Everywhere, it seems, inch marks (") are being substituted for open (") and close (") quotation marks, and foot marks (') are substituted for apostrophes (').

To use the right characters, some software requires that you use special keystrokes. Others can be set automatically so that the computer will insert the correct characters. (The computer guesses which characters you want based on context, and it usually guesses right.)

Using true typographical characters is a small detail, but it has a larger psychological impact: It is an accumulation of small differences that subconsciously signal a reader that a document (and by association, what the document says) is the work of a professional and not of an amateur.

21. Make type stand out against its background.

Readability depends on the contrast between letters and their background; if you reduce contrast then you reduce readability. You don't have to print everything in black ink on white paper, but be careful when you don't.

A lot of word processors and desktop publishing programs can create gray shading using a small dot pat-

**Make type stand out
against its background.**
If you use a tint, make
sure it is dark enough
or light enough to
retain readability. In
these examples, black
type and white type are
shown against 10%,
30%, 60%, and 90%
tints.

General statement of purpose: To develop, guide and coordinate company communication via four means: news media, advertising, publication of sales literature, and direct presentation.

General statement of purpose: To develop, guide and coordinate company communication via four means: news media, advertising, publication of sales literature, and direct presentation.

General statement of purpose: To develop, guide and coordinate company communication via four means: news media, advertising, publication of sales literature, and direct presentation.

General statement of purpose: To develop, guide and coordinate company communication via four means: news media, advertising, publication of sales literature, and direct presentation.

and their background; if you reduce contrast then you reduce readability. You don't have to print everything in black ink on white paper, but be careful when you don't.

A lot of word processors and desktop publishing programs can create gray shading using a small dot pattern called a *tint*. The darkness of the shading is expressed by its percentage: A 50 percent tint means that within the shaded portion, half of the paper is covered with the small dots; a 25 percent tint means that only a quarter of the paper is covered with dots. A 10 percent tint, then, is a light gray, while a 90 percent tint larger than type against a white background to be as readable.

Never print a font over a tint unless it is at least 10-point type—and it should probably be larger. If you are using black type over a tint, the tint should probably not be stronger than 20 percent. If you are using white type over a tint, the tint should be at least 50 percent. In both cases, avoid thin typefaces—they won't show up well enough. (Note that the italics in some fonts are much thinner than the font's normal style and shouldn't be used over tints.)

If you're sending your document out to a printer and are using color, be careful about the color you use for type. A light color of ink may look wonderful as a large swatch but may be illegible when printed as a 9-point font. The smaller the type, the more likely it is that it should be printed in dark shades.

22. Don't print text over photos or illustrations.

A common design effect is to print words across an image such as a photograph or illustration. If the area of the image is light and the font is large enough and bold enough to stand out, this technique can help to combine the words and the pictures into a unified visual presentation (see Rule 9). It's not a good idea if there's any question at all about the readability of the words. This is especially true in the case of printing columns of text directly over an image.

Although this is a common and sometimes dramatic technique in consumer magazines, it's not a good idea for business. Your reader won't be able to read the text easily or see the picture clearly. The only exception to this rule is when a large portion of an image is white or nearly white—a light sky or a large snow bank, for example.

Don't "tombstone" headlines. Headlines set next to each other can cause readers to misread them as one long headline (sometimes resulting in odd meanings).

Fun Time To Be Had at Employee Picnic

This year's Fourth of July employee picnic will once again be open to all employees at no charge. Everyone is invited to meet at Brookside Park and to bring their families. Hot dogs and soda will be served, there will be games for the kids and even a basketball tournament between the PDQ HoopMasters

When Boredom Hits in Your Office

There's no denying it: no matter how challenging our job is, no matter how interesting the work, no matter how stimulating our coworkers, we all face boredom on the job at one time or another. The question is, what to do when it strikes?

Psychology experts suggest that boredom seldom arises

The solution is to separate the stories and their headlines, as shown here.

Fun Time To Be Had at Employee Picnic

This year's Fourth of July employee picnic will once again be open to all employees at no charge. Everyone is invited to meet at Brookside Park and to bring their families. Hot dogs and soda will be served. There will be games for the kids and even a basketball tournament between the PDQ HoopMasters and the Court Jesters.

When Boredom Hits in Your Office

There's no denying it: no matter how challenging our job is, no matter how interesting the work, no matter how stimulating our coworkers, we all face boredom on the job at one time or another. The question is, what to do when it strikes?

Psychology experts suggest that boredom seldom arises from the

23. Don't "tombstone" headlines.

This is a time-honored rule of newspaper layout, and applies if your document has multiple columns, stories, and headlines on a single page. To tombstone headlines means to place the headlines of different stories next to each other—the danger is that your reader will read across both headlines.

If you have to put two headlines right next to each other, and they need to be the same size, make them short (creating a break of white space between them) or set one in a different style—bold, for example.

Guide Your Reader

IN THIS SECTION we begin to talk about your document as a whole. Now that you know your message and audience, have chosen a form for your document, and have chosen your fonts and learned the basics of using them, you need to put these parts together to create a document that provides maximum communication.

Although the principles in this chapter work for any kind of document, many of them are most easily applied to multiple-column documents. The advantage of a multiple-column layout is that it gives you more flexibility to combine visual components—headlines, text, and images—on one page, which increases their emotional and communication impact. This combination is also more powerful because it engages the reader by offering a choice of what to look at on the page first.

But with this increased opportunity comes increased responsibility. While you want to offer your reader choices, you don't want one of those choices to be to ignore part of your message. The problem then becomes how to combine the different components into a single layout that both actively engages the reader and guides the reader to absorb your ideas in the proper order. To accomplish this, you need to think systematically, analyzing and controlling all the visual aspects of your material. That is what this section is about.

Some of the suggestions in this section might be beyond the ability of a word processor. If you will be producing a lot of complex documents, it's a good idea to buy fully featured desktop publishing software.

24. Show what deserves first attention, second attention, and so forth.

The goal of document design is to order information in a way that speeds it into the reader's mind. The first step of this process is to divide your message into logical parts. The next step is to show the relationship among these parts.

In a simple document, such as a report that uses only text, headlines, and subheads, your reader's path is already controlled. He will begin at the beginning and read each page from top to bottom. Even if he skims your document, his path can still be thought of as a direct route.

In this case, you show the relationship among the parts of your information by deciding what order the parts will appear in, and whether they begin with a large headline, a smaller headline, a subhead, or a bullet, or are simply part of the running text (see Rule 6).

In more complicated documents that are composed of several columns and include headlines, photos, charts, diagrams, and other graphics, you must create a visual path for the reader: You must show him what to look at first, second, and third.

You might think that the simplest way to do this would be to just insert your photo or chart into the reading flow. But this doesn't work. The reason it doesn't is because the nature of an image—the way it communicates its information—is entirely different from words. We read words, but we look at images. Once your reader begins looking at your page, he is no longer reading it, and is free to look at whatever he wants to. You must guide his attention with visual cues, showing him what *you* think should be looked at first, second, and third. I call this creating a *hierarchy of attention.*

The Five Qualities
of a Hierarchy of Attention

There are five qualities you can manipulate to create a hierarchy of attention: *size, contrast, position, form,* and *content.*

Size The largest item on a page is the first thing a reader sees and is what he will generally consider the most important.

As size decreases, so does perceived importance. The most straightforward way to create a hierarchy of attention is to make essential words or pictures largest, and to size all others according to their relative value. The most obvious example of this technique is your local newspaper: Important stories get big headlines and pictures.

Because size is the most powerful quality, you should consider it first. To use it effectively, you can't have too many things the same size. If you're producing a newsletter or brochure, try making your lead picture or headline at least twice as big as anything else on the page. Then you can set sizes for the other items, creating three or four headline or photo sizes. Don't pick too many; for example, don't have ten headlines that are ten different sizes—instead of having a hierarchy with a few clear levels, you'll have mush (see Rule 25).

In simpler documents, such as memos, resumes, and reports, you should use size more modestly. Size is the

The five qualities of a hierarchy of attention

1. Size Larger items command more attention and are seen as more important. In this case, the large headline delivers the primary news while the subhead adds detail.

Harding Industries Acquires Nascom
The Electronic Giant Diversifies

In September, 1994, recalls James Harding, chief executive of the electronic giant Harding Industries, sales had gone south. Already under pressure from hundreds of new players in the volatile video game market, Harding had nothing to lose by taking a big new risk. "It was frightening," Harding recalls, "but there was nothing else to do. And it's turned out well so far."

The fearful time paid off. Harding surprised everyone—including Wall Street—with a first-quarter profit of $3.5 million. Many attribute that to the CEO's canny acquisition of Nascom earlier in the year.

In September, 1994, recalls James Harding, chief executive of the electronic giant Harding Industries, sales had gone south. Already under pressure from hundreds of new players in the volatile video game market, Harding had nothing to lose by taking a big new risk. "It was frightening, Harding recalls, "but there was nothing else to do. And it's turned out well so far."

The fearful time paid off. Harding surprised everyone—including Wall Street—with a first-quarter profit of $3.5 million. Many attribute that to the CEO's canny acquisition of Nascom earlier in the year.

In September, 1994, recalls James Harding, chief executive of the electronic giant Harding Industries, sales had gone south. Already under pressure from hundreds of new players in the volatile video game market, Harding had nothing to lose by taking a big new risk. "It was frightening, Harding recalls, "but there was nothing else to do. And it's turned out well so far."

The fearful time paid off. Harding surprised everyone—including Wall Street—with a first-quarter profit of $3.5 million. Many attribute that to the CEO's canny acquisition of Nascom earlier in the year.

In September, 1994, recalls James Harding, chief executive of the electronic giant Harding Industries, sales had gone south. Already under pressure from hundreds of new players in the volatile video game market, Harding had nothing to lose by taking a big new risk. "It was frightening, Harding recalls, "but there was nothing else to do. And it's turned out well so far."

The fearful time paid off. Harding surprised everyone—including Wall

Street—with a first-quarter profit of $3.5 million. Many attribute that to the CEO's canny acquisition of Nascom earlier in the year.

In September, 1994, recalls James Harding, chief executive of the electronic giant Harding Industries, sales had gone south. Already under pressure from hundreds of new players in the volatile video game market, Harding had nothing to lose by taking a big new risk. "It was frightening," Harding recalls, "but there was nothing else to do. And it's turned out well so far."

The fearful time paid off. Harding surprised everyone—including Wall Street—with a first-quarter profit of $3.5 million. Many attribute that to the CEO's canny acquisition of Nascom earlier in the year.

In September, 1994, recalls James Harding, chief executive of the electronic giant Harding Industries, sales had gone south. Already under pressure from hundreds of new players in the volatile video game market, Harding had nothing to lose by taking a big new risk. "It was frightening, Harding recalls, "but there was nothing else to do. And it's turned out well so far."

The fearful time paid off. Harding surprised everyone—including Wall Street—with a first-quarter profit of $3.5 million. Many attribute that to the CEO's canny acquisition of Nascom earlier in the year.

In September, 1994, recalls James Harding, chief executive of the electronic giant Harding Industries, sales had gone south. Already under pressure from hundreds of new players in the volatile video game market, Harding had nothing to lose by taking a big new risk. "It was frightening, Harding recalls, "but there was

nothing else to do. And it's turned out well so far."

The fearful time paid off. Harding surprised everyone—including Wall Street—with a first-quarter profit of $3.5 million. Many attribute that to the CEO's canny acquisition of Nascom earlier in the year.

In September, 1994, recalls James Harding, chief executive of the electronic giant Harding Industries, sales had gone south. Already under pressure from hundreds of new players in the volatile video game market, Harding had nothing to lose by taking a big new risk. "It was frightening," Harding recalls, "but there was nothing else to do. And it's turned out well so far."

The fearful time paid off. Harding surprised everyone—including Wall Street—with a first-quarter profit of $3.5 million. Many attribute that to the CEO's canny acquisition of Nascom earlier in the year.

In September, 1994, recalls James Harding, chief executive of the electronic giant Harding Industries, sales had gone south. Already under pressure from hundreds of new players in the volatile video game market, Harding had nothing to lose by taking a big new risk. "It was frightening, Harding recalls, "but there was nothing else to do. And it's turned out well so far."

The fearful time paid off. Harding surprised everyone—including Wall Street—with a first-quarter profit of $3.5 million. Many attribute that to the CEO's canny acquisition of Nascom earlier in the year.

In September, 1994, recalls James Harding, chief executive of the electronic giant Harding Industries, sales had gone south. Already under pressure from hundreds of new players in

least sophisticated of the five qualities: Too much size (that is, too great a difference between the smaller and larger items) in these more conservative documents is overkill.

In a resume, for example, you may want your name to be the largest item on the page—but it doesn't need to be twice as large as the other items. Moreover, you probably shouldn't use more than two or three sizes of fonts for a resume. Instead, concentrate on working with the other four qualities to create a subtle hierarchy of attention that organizes your information for clarity and readability.

2. Contrast. An item that is darker or lighter than a similar item will stand out; that which is darker is usually seen as more important. Here, the more important headline was set in extra bold.

Harding Industries Acquires Nascom
The Electronic Giant Diversifies

In September, 1994, recalls James Harding, chief executive of the electronic giant Harding Industries, sales had gone south. Already under pressure from hundreds of new players in the volatile video game market, Harding had nothing to lose by taking a big new risk. "It was frightening," Harding recalls, "but there was nothing else to do. And it's turned out well so far."

The fearful time paid off. Harding surprised everyone—including Wall Street—with a first-quarter profit of $3.5 million. Many attribute that to the CEO's canny acquisition of Nascom earlier in the year.

In September, 1994, recalls James Harding, chief executive of the electronic giant Harding Industries, sales had gone south. Already under pressure from hundreds of new players in the volatile video game market, Harding had nothing to lose by taking a big new risk. "It was frightening," Harding recalls, "but there was nothing else to do. And it's turned out well so far."

The fearful time paid off. Harding surprised everyone—including Wall Street—with a first-quarter profit of $3.5 million. Many attribute that to the CEO's canny acquisition of Nascom earlier in the year.

In September, 1994, recalls James Harding, chief executive of the electronic giant Harding Industries, sales had gone south. Already under pressure from hundreds of new players in the volatile video game market, Harding had nothing to lose by taking a big new risk. "It was frightening," Harding recalls, "but there was nothing else to do. And it's turned out well so far."

The fearful time paid off. Harding surprised everyone—including Wall

Street—with a first-quarter profit of $3.5 million. Many attribute that to the CEO's canny acquisition of Nascom earlier in the year.

In September, 1994, recalls James Harding, chief executive of the electronic giant Harding Industries, sales had gone south. Already under pressure from hundreds of new players in the volatile video game market, Harding had nothing to lose by taking a big new risk. "It was frightening," Harding recalls, "but there was nothing else to do. And it's turned out well so far."

The fearful time paid off. Harding surprised everyone—including Wall Street—with a first-quarter profit of $3.5 million. Many attribute that to the CEO's canny acquisition of Nascom earlier in the year.

In September, 1994, recalls James Harding, chief executive of the electronic giant Harding Industries, sales had gone south. Already under pressure from hundreds of new players in the volatile video game market, Harding had nothing to lose by taking a big new risk. "It was frightening," Harding recalls, "but there was

nothing else to do. And it's turned out well so far."

The fearful time paid off. Harding surprised everyone—including Wall Street—with a first-quarter profit of $3.5 million. Many attribute that to the CEO's canny acquisition of Nascom earlier in the year.

In September, 1994, recalls James Harding, chief executive of the electronic giant Harding Industries, sales had gone south. Already under pressure from hundreds of new players in the volatile video game market, Harding had nothing to lose by taking a big new risk. "It was frightening," Harding recalls, "but there was nothing else to do. And it's turned out well so far."

The fearful time paid off. Harding surprised everyone—including Wall Street—with a first-quarter profit of $3.5 million. Many attribute that to the CEO's canny acquisition of Nascom earlier in the year.

In September, 1994, recalls James Harding, chief executive of the electronic giant Harding Industries, sales had gone south. Already under pressure from hundreds of new players in

Contrast Whatever is lighter or darker than its background or other items becomes more noticeable.

A bold headline, for example, will normally command more attention than a medium headline if the two are the same size. But if a page is filled with bold headlines, and one is medium, then the medium one will stand out. In general, though, whatever's bolder is perceived as more important.

You can use contrast to fine-tune a hierarchy you've set up using size. In a newsletter, let's say you have four different headline sizes. Two of the stories are of nearly the same importance, and will be placed next to each other, yet you want one to receive a little less emphasis. Use contrast by making one headline bold, the other medium. You can also use contrast to balance a headline with a subhead that accompanies it. In this situation, it may be hard to balance their relative importance: The subhead may be nearly as important as the headline to you. In this case you can use contrast by making the headline medium and the subhead bold—but keep the headline somewhat larger than the subhead. To use contrast in text, see Rules 7 and 8.

Position A reader's eye falls first to the visual center of the page, then (in Western cultures) scans left to right and top to bottom. So your reader will see whatever is in the upper left corner before he sees something in the lower right.

This is a powerful tendency: If something in the visual center of a page is interesting enough, your reader may continue down and never return. Advertising authority David Ogilvy found that when a photograph is placed below the text in advertising, readership of the text drops by 10 percent because people look at the photograph and then turn the page, instead of going back up to find the text.

To realize how powerful positioning can be, consider the real-life situation of stocking grocery shelves. One study of supermarket merchandising found that goods on eye-level shelves far outsold others. When those same products were put on waist-level shelves, sales dropped 26 percent. When they were put on the bottom shelves, sales plummeted by 43 percent. If you place your key ideas at the floor level of your document, you can expect a similar result.

The more involved a reader is with a document, the more likely will be his tendency to look first at the left-hand side rather than to scan the middle. If you're writing a letter to solicit clients that will go out to a cold list—that is, people who don't know your company—you should center the subheads that divide your paragraphs because your reader will probably scan down the center of the page to see if there's anything of interest. If you're writing a report to your boss, put the heads and subheads on the left—she'll be reading all of it (you trust), so placing the heads there will make them read faster and seem more immediate.

Poorly positioned text can cause an irritating pause in the absorption of information. For example, compare these three ways of positioning this information:

President	Melanie Havens
Vice President	Scott Ray
Director of Operations	Judy Berenson

President..Melanie Havens
Vice President..Scott Ray
Director of Operations ....Judy Berenson

President: Melanie Havens
Vice President: Scott Ray
Director of Operations: Judy Berenson

In the first example, the reader senses a gap between one piece of information and the next. The gap is exaggerated because it takes a moment for the reader's eye to locate what on the left goes with what on the right.

The second example is better: The items are closer together and the dots in between (called *leader dots*) guide the eye.

The third example is the best. Because this is a short list, there is no reason to separate the items at all. The

3. Position. In Western cultures, people read from left to right, top to bottom, so an item in the upper left corner of a page will be noticed before something in the lower right. In this example, the more important headline is placed in the primary position.

Harding Industries Acquires Nascom

In September, 1994, recalls James Harding, chief executive of the electronic giant Harding Industries, sales had gone south. Already under pressure from hundreds of new players in the volatile video game market, Harding had nothing to lose by taking a big new risk. "It was frightening," Harding recalls, "but there was nothing else to do. And it's turned out well so far."

The fearful time paid off. Harding surprised everyone—including Wall Street—with a first-quarter profit of $3.5 million. Many attribute that to the CEO's canny acquisition of Nascom earlier in the year.

In September, 1994, recalls James Harding, chief executive of the electronic giant Harding Industries, sales had gone south. Already under pressure from hundreds of new players in the volatile video game market, Harding had nothing to lose by taking a big new risk. "It was frightening," Harding recalls, "but there was nothing else to do. And it's turned out well so far."

The fearful time paid off. Harding surprised everyone—including Wall Street—with a first-quarter profit of $3.5 million. Many attribute that to the CEO's canny acquisition of Nascom earlier in the year.

In September, 1994, recalls James Harding, chief executive of the electronic giant Harding Industries, sales had gone south. Already under pressure from hundreds of new players in the volatile video game market, Harding had nothing to lose by taking a big new risk. "It was frightening," Harding recalls, "but there was nothing else to do. And it's turned out well so far."

The fearful time paid off. Harding surprised everyone—including Wall Street—with a first-quarter profit of $3.5 million. Many attribute that to the CEO's canny acquisition of Nascom earlier in the year.

In September, 1994, recalls James Harding, chief executive of the electronic giant Harding Industries, sales had gone south. Already under pressure from hundreds of new players in the volatile video game market, Harding had nothing to lose by taking a big new risk. "It was frightening," Harding recalls, "but there was nothing else to do. And it's turned out well so far."

In September, 1994, recalls James Harding, chief executive of the electronic giant Harding Industries, sales had gone south. Already under pressure from hundreds of new players in the volatile video game market, Harding had nothing to lose by taking a big new risk. "It was frightening," Harding recalls, "but there was nothing else to do. And it's turned out well so far."

The fearful time paid off. Harding surprised everyone—including Wall Street—with a first-quarter profit of $3.5 million. Many attribute that to the CEO's canny acquisition of Nascom earlier in the year.

In September, 1994, recalls James Harding, chief executive of the electronic giant Harding Industries, sales had gone south. Already under pressure from hundreds of new players in the volatile video game market, Harding had nothing to lose by taking a big new risk. "It was frightening," Harding recalls, "but there was nothing else to do. And it's turned out well so far."

The fearful time paid off. Harding surprised everyone—including Wall Street—with a first-quarter profit of $3.5 million. Many attribute that to

the CEO's canny acquisition of Nascom earlier in the year.

In September, 1994, recalls James Harding, chief executive of the electronic giant Harding Industries, sales had gone south. Already under pressure from hundreds of new players in the volatile video game market, Harding had nothing to lose by taking a big new risk. "It was frightening," Harding recalls, "but there was nothing else to do. And it's turned out well so far."

The fearful time paid off. Harding surprised everyone—including Wall Street—with a first-quarter profit of $3.5 million. Many attribute that to the CEO's canny acquisition of Nascom earlier in the year.

In September, 1994, recalls James Harding, chief executive of the electronic giant Harding Industries, sales had gone south. Already under pressure from hundreds of new players in the volatile video game market, Harding had nothing to lose by taking a big new risk. "It was frightening," Harding recalls, "but there was nothing else to do. And it's turned out well so far."

The fearful time paid off. Harding surprised everyone—including Wall

The Electronic Giant Diversifies

In September, 1994, recalls James Harding, chief executive of the electronic giant Harding Industries, sales had gone south. Already under pressure from hundreds of new players in the volatile video game market, Harding had nothing to lose by taking a big new risk. "It was frightening," Harding recalls, "but there was nothing else to do. And it's turned out well so far."

The fearful time paid off. Harding

surprised everyone—including Wall Street—with a first-quarter profit of $3.5 million. Many attribute that to the CEO's canny acquisition of Nascom earlier in the year.

In September, 1994, recalls James Harding, chief executive of the electronic giant Harding Industries, sales had gone south. Already under pressure from hundreds of new players in the volatile video game market, Harding had nothing to lose by taking

technique of separating items on the left and right, with leader dots in the middle, should be reserved for long lists where your reader is likely to need to skim the left-hand side before ever moving to the right (such as in a phone book). In this case, isolating the reference on the left helps because the items are easier to scan.

Position also has an effect in multipage documents. When a reader turns a page, he will most often look to the page revealed first—the right-hand page—and then look back to the left to see the other page. This is why advertisers in magazines often ask for a right-hand page position. If you're creating a brochure that unfolds,

4. Form. Readers notice an item that is picture-like before words because it can be "read" faster. Even though the headlines and the illustration in this example take up approximately equal space, readers will notice the picture first because of its form.

Harding Industries Acquires Nascom
The Electronic Giant Diversifies

In September, 1994, recalls James Harding, chief executive of the electronic giant Harding Industries, sales had gone south. Already under pressure from hundreds of new players in the volatile video game market, Harding had nothing to lose by taking a big new risk. "It was frightening," Harding recalls, "but there was nothing else to do. And it's turned out well so far."

The fearful time paid off. Harding surprised everyone—including Wall Street—with a first-quarter profit of $3.5 million. Many attribute that to the CEO's canny acquisition of Nascom earlier in the year.

In September, 1994, recalls James Harding, chief executive of the electronic giant Harding Industries, sales had gone south. Already under pressure from hundreds of new players in the volatile video game market, Harding had nothing to lose by taking a big new risk. "It was frightening," Harding recalls, "but there was nothing else to do. And it's turned out well so far."

The fearful time paid off. Harding surprised everyone—including Wall Street—with a first-quarter profit of $3.5 million. Many attribute that to the CEO's canny acquisition of Nascom earlier in the year.

In September, 1994, recalls James Harding, chief executive of the electronic giant Harding Industries, sales had gone south. Already under pressure from hundreds of new players in the volatile video game market, Harding had nothing to lose by taking a big new risk. "It was frightening," Harding recalls, "but there was nothing else to do. And it's turned out well so far."

The fearful time paid off. Harding surprised everyone—including Wall

Street—with a first-quarter profit of $3.5 million. Many attribute that to the CEO's canny acquisition of

Nascom earlier in the year.

In September, 1994, recalls James Harding, chief executive of the electronic giant Harding Industries, sales had gone south. Already under pressure from hundreds of new players in the volatile video game market, Harding had nothing to lose by taking a big new risk. "It was frightening," Harding recalls, "but there was nothing else to do. And it's turned out well so far."

The fearful time paid off. Harding surprised everyone—including Wall Street—with a first-quarter profit of $3.5 million. Many attribute that to the CEO's canny acquisition of Nascom earlier in the year.

In September, 1994, recalls James Harding, chief executive of the electronic giant Harding Industries, sales had gone south. Already under pressure from hundreds of new players in the volatile video game market,

Harding had nothing to lose by taking a big new risk. "It was frightening," Harding recalls, "but there was nothing else to do. And it's turned out well so far."

The fearful time paid off. Harding surprised everyone—including Wall Street—with a first-quarter profit of $3.5 million. Many attribute that to the CEO's canny acquisition of Nascom earlier in the year.

In September, 1994, recalls James Harding, chief executive of the electronic giant Harding Industries, sales had gone south. Already under pressure from hundreds of new players in the volatile video game market, Harding had nothing to lose by taking a big new risk. "It was frightening," Harding recalls, "but there was nothing else to do. And it's turned out well so far."

The fearful time paid off. Harding surprised everyone—including Wall Street—with a first-quarter profit of $3.5 million. Many attribute that to the CEO's canny acquisition of Nascom earlier in the year.

In September, 1994, recalls James Harding, chief executive of the elec-

remember that the right-hand side of any spread will get the reader's first attention.

Form Form—that is, whether an item is a headline, a graph, a diagram, or a photo—strongly influences attention. People will see anything picture-like first because it doesn't require the extra step of reading. To make a headline as compelling as a chart, you must compensate by making the headline larger or putting it in a more prominent position.

If you're putting sales charts in a report, but you think the flat sales lines don't tell the whole story, top the page with a very large headline (and maybe a sub-head too, if the news is really bad) and put the charts in the bottom right-hand corner to force your reader to see your words first. That way you have a chance to explain the results.

Content What a headline, chart, or photo says can command extra attention out of proportion to its size, relative contrast, position, or form. Direct mail advertisers have found, for example, that the words *free* and *new* attract special attention. Photos of people generally attract more attention than photos of anything else, and close-ups attract more attention than more distant shots.

To determine the natural hierarchy of attention between graphic items you must estimate the combined strength of the item's form (discussed above) and its content. Here's a rough approximation of how form and content combine to draw our attention, from the most attention-getting items to the least:

Close-up photos of people, such as portraits

Longer views of people, such as a group shot

Realistic illustrations of people

Cartoons of people

Close-up photographs of inanimate objects

Longer views of objects, or complicated photos

Illustrative charts (sometimes called infographics)

Common charts (such as pie charts or bar charts)

Uncommon charts

A major influencing factor is the personal involvement the reader has with the content, and you should con-

5. Content. The content of a message can give it more attention-power than it would normally receive based on its other qualities. In this case, if your readers are stockholders in Harding Industries, the subhead "Stockholders Reap Huge Return" would draw more attention than the headline.

Harding Industries Acquires Nascom
Stockholders Reap Huge Return

In September, 1994, recalls James Harding, chief executive of the electronic giant Harding Industries, sales had gone south. Already under pressure from hundreds of new players in the volatile video game market, Harding had nothing to lose by taking a big new risk. "It was frightening," Harding recalls, "but there was nothing else to do. And it's turned out well so far."

The fearful time paid off. Harding surprised everyone—including Wall Street—with a first-quarter profit of $3.5 million. Many attribute that to the CEO's canny acquisition of Nascom earlier in the year.

In September, 1994, recalls James Harding, chief executive of the electronic giant Harding Industries, sales had gone south. Already under pressure from hundreds of new players in the volatile video game market, Harding had nothing to lose by taking a big new risk. "It was frightening," Harding recalls, "but there was nothing else to do. And it's turned out well so far."

The fearful time paid off. Harding surprised everyone—including Wall Street—with a first-quarter profit of $3.5 million. Many attribute that to the CEO's canny acquisition of Nascom earlier in the year.

In September, 1994, recalls James Harding, chief executive of the electronic giant Harding Industries, sales had gone south. Already under pressure from hundreds of new players in the volatile video game market, Harding had nothing to lose by taking a big new risk. "It was frightening," Harding recalls, "but there was nothing else to do. And it's turned out well so far."

The fearful time paid off. Harding surprised everyone—including Wall Street—with a first-quarter profit of $3.5 million. Many attribute that to the CEO's canny acquisition of Nascom earlier in the year.

In September, 1994, recalls James Harding, chief executive of the electronic giant Harding Industries, sales had gone south. Already under pressure from hundreds of new players in the volatile video game market, Harding had nothing to lose by taking a big new risk. "It was frightening," Harding recalls, "but there was nothing else to do. And it's turned out well so far."

The fearful time paid off. Harding surprised everyone—including Wall Street—with a first-quarter profit of $3.5 million. Many attribute that to the CEO's canny acquisition of Nascom earlier in the year.

In September, 1994, recalls James Harding, chief executive of the electronic giant Harding Industries, sales had gone south. Already under pressure from hundreds of new players in the volatile video game market, Harding had nothing to lose by taking a big new risk. "It was frightening," Harding recalls, "but there was nothing else to do. And it's turned out well so far."

The fearful time paid off. Harding surprised everyone—including Wall Street—with a first-quarter profit of $3.5 million. Many attribute that to the CEO's canny acquisition of Nascom earlier in the year.

In September, 1994, recalls James Harding, chief executive of the electronic giant Harding Industries, sales had gone south. Already under pressure from hundreds of new players in the volatile video game market, Harding had nothing to lose by taking a big new risk. "It was frightening," Harding recalls, "but there was

nothing else to do. And it's turned out well so far."

The fearful time paid off. Harding surprised everyone—including Wall Street—with a first-quarter profit of $3.5 million. Many attribute that to the CEO's canny acquisition of Nascom earlier in the year.

In September, 1994, recalls James Harding, chief executive of the electronic giant Harding Industries, sales had gone south. Already under pressure from hundreds of new players in the volatile video game market, Harding had nothing to lose by taking a big new risk. "It was frightening," Harding recalls, "but there was nothing else to do. And it's turned out well so far."

The fearful time paid off. Harding surprised everyone—including Wall Street—with a first-quarter profit of $3.5 million. Many attribute that to the CEO's canny acquisition of Nascom earlier in the year.

In September, 1994, recalls James Harding, chief executive of the electronic giant Harding Industries, sales had gone south. Already under pressure from hundreds of new players in the volatile video game market, Harding had nothing to lose by taking a big new risk. "It was frightening," Harding recalls, "but there was nothing else to do. And it's turned out well so far."

The fearful time paid off. Harding surprised everyone—including Wall Street—with a first-quarter profit of $3.5 million. Many attribute that to the CEO's canny acquisition of Nascom earlier in the year.

In September, 1994, recalls James Harding, chief executive of the electronic giant Harding Industries, sales had gone south. Already under pressure from hundreds of new players in

sider this carefully in your design. For example, if you're designing a report, and you know that everyone will be looking for the end-of-year summary chart, you don't need to worry about featuring it. Use the other four qualities—size, contrast, position, and form—to boost the level of the other messages in your document. You can put the summary chart in a relatively low level of your hierarchy of attention, knowing people will find it anyway. This is one reason most annual reports put the financial numbers in the back while the material that highlights the company's accomplishments is featured in front.

How to use a hierarchy of attention to emphasize parts of a story

In this layout, the importance of acquisition to the stockholders is stressed while the role of the CEO is reduced.

The **form** of the message "Stockholders Reap Huge Return" has been changed from words to an eye-catching graphic.

The **size** of the headline is large, to stress its message.

The **size** of the CEO's portrait is small and in a less powerful **position.** Parts of the portrait have also been cropped out, reducing the amount of **content.**

Shareholders' Earnings

July '94
$14.4 million

June,'94
$10 million

Harding Industries Acquires Nascom

The Electronic Giant Diversifies

In September, 1994, recalls James Harding, chief executive of the electronic giant Harding Industries, sales had gone south. Already under pressure from hundreds of new players in the volatile video game market, Harding had nothing to lose by taking a big new risk. "It was frightening," Harding recalls, "but there was nothing else to do. And it's turned out well so far."

The fearful time paid off. Harding surprised everyone—including Wall Street—with a first-quarter profit of $3.5 million. Many attribute that to the CEO's canny acquisition of Nascom earlier in the year.

In September, 1994, recalls James Harding, chief executive of the electronic giant Harding Industries, sales had gone south. Already under pressure from hundreds of new players in the volatile video game market, Harding had nothing to lose by taking a big new risk. "It was frightening," Harding recalls, "but there was nothing else to do. And it's turned out well so far."

The fearful time paid off. Harding surprised everyone—including Wall Street—with a first-quarter profit of $3.5 million. Many attribute that to the CEO's canny acquisition of

Nascom earlier in the year.

In September, 1994, recalls James Harding, chief executive of the electronic giant Harding Industries, sales had gone south. Already under pressure from hundreds of new players in the volatile video game market, Harding had nothing to lose by taking a big new risk. "It was frightening," Harding recalls, "but there was nothing else to do. And it's turned out well so far."

The fearful time paid off. Harding surprised everyone—including Wall Street—with a first-quarter profit of $3.5 million. Many attribute that to the CEO's canny acquisition of Nascom earlier in the year.

In September, 1994, recalls James Harding, chief executive of the electronic giant Harding Industries, sales had gone south. Already under pressure from hundreds of new players in the volatile video game market, Harding had nothing to lose by taking a big new risk. "It was frightening," Harding recalls, "but there was nothing else to do. And it's turned out well so far."

CEO James Harding

The fearful time paid off. Harding surprised everyone—including Wall Street—with a first-quarter profit of $3.5 million. Many attribute that to the CEO's canny acquisition of Nascom earlier in the year.

In September, 1994, recalls James Harding, chief executive of the electronic giant Harding Industries, sales had gone south. Already under pressure from hundreds of new players in the volatile video game market, Harding had nothing to lose by taking a big new risk. "It was frightening," Harding recalls, "but there was nothing else to do. And it's turned out well so far."

The fearful time paid off. Harding surprised everyone—including Wall Street—with a first-quarter profit of $3.5 million. Many attribute that to the CEO's canny acquisition of Nascom earlier in the year.

In September, 1994, recalls James Harding, chief executive of the electronic giant Harding Industries, sales had gone south. Already under pressure from hundreds of new players in the volatile video game market, Harding had nothing to lose by taking a big new risk. "It was frightening," Harding recalls, "but there was nothing else to do. And it's turned

---

Creating a Hierarchy of Attention

To show your reader what to look at first, second, and so forth, you need to plan your hierarchy of attention. The first step is to evaluate the components of your message. You can usually change the size, contrast, and position of your components because most of your message is normally expressed in words that can be made large or small, bold or medium, and so forth.

Sometimes you can change the form of your message. You may be able to show something in a chart instead of describing it in words. You may also be able

Here the CEO is seen as the primary force behind the acquision. Even the headline now seems to refer to him because of the **size** and **position** of the items.

The CEO's name is now in a very prominent **position.**

The **content, size** and **position** of the portrait have been boosted in the hierarchy

The **size** of the old headline has been reduced to a subhead and distinguished from the other subhead with **contrast;** the **size** of the old subhead has been increased to become the headline.

CEO James Harding

The Electronic Giant Diversifies

Harding Industries Acquires Nascom

Shareholders Reap Huge Returns

In September, 1994, recalls James Harding, chief executive of the electronic giant Harding Industries, sales had gone south. Already under pressure from hundreds of new players in the volatile video game market, Harding had nothing to lose by taking a big new risk. "It was frightening," Harding recalls, "but there was nothing else to do. And it's turned out well so far."

The fearful time paid off. Harding surprised everyone—including Wall Street—with a first-quarter profit of $3.5 million. Many attribute that to the CEO's canny acquisition of Nascom earlier in the year.

In September, 1994, recalls James Harding, chief executive of the electronic giant Harding Industries, sales had gone south. Already under pressure from hundreds of new players in the volatile video game market, Harding had nothing to lose by tak-

ing a big new risk. "It was frightening," Harding recalls, "but there was nothing else to do. And it's turned out well so far."

The fearful time paid off. Harding surprised everyone—including Wall Street—with a first-quarter profit of $3.5 million. Many attribute that to the CEO's canny acquisition of Nascom earlier in the year.

In September, 1994, recalls James Harding, chief executive of the electronic giant Harding Industries, sales had gone south. Already under pressure from hundreds of new players in the volatile video game market, Harding had nothing to lose by taking a big new risk. "It was frightening," Harding recalls, "but there was nothing else to do. And it's turned out well so far."

The fearful time paid off. Harding surprised everyone—including Wall Street—with a first-quarter profit of

$3.5 million. Many attribute that to the CEO's canny acquisition of Nascom earlier in the year.

In September, 1994, recalls James Harding, chief executive of the electronic giant Harding Industries, sales had gone south. Already under pressure from hundreds of new players in the volatile video game market, Harding had nothing to lose by taking a big new risk. "It was frightening," Harding recalls, "but there was nothing else to do. And it's turned out well so far."

The fearful time paid off. Harding surprised everyone—including Wall Street—with a first-quarter profit of $3.5 million. Many attribute that to the CEO's canny acquisition of Nascom earlier in the year.

In September, 1994, recalls James Harding, chief executive of the electronic giant Harding Industries, sales had gone south. Already under pres-

to change the content of your message, deciding to feature one product instead of another.

Once the form and content of your message are set you can decide where each item should fall in the hierarchy, keeping in mind that picture-like forms have a natural advantage. Use size and position to arrange the items to create a rough hierarchy. Make final adjustments using contrast and refinements in position and size. Remember that empty space is an item on your page (see Rule 27), and although it doesn't have content or form, its size, position, and contrast can be adjusted with other items.

25. Create only the number of visually distinct levels you need.

Although most people don't approach the design of a document using the idea of a hierarchy of attention, they do realize that some parts of their message should be emphasized. But a problem often develops because in an effort to draw the reader's attention to everything in the document, nothing is emphasized. In a flyer, for example, you might make the headline and store name bold and position them near the top of the page. You look again and decide that the sale products aren't prominent enough, so you increase the point size and put them in italic. Then you decide that the sale dates are very important, so you underline them. Next you think that the store's address is essential, so you increase its size. Soon there is no hierarchy at all—every part of the message is fighting for the top level.

Another problem that happens is when you realize that there must be a hierarchy, but you try to create too many levels. In this case, using the same flyer as an example, let's say the headline and store name are both in 72-point boldface. You feel the sale products are only slightly less important than the headline, so you put them in 68-point boldface. You go on to put the sale dates in 65-point boldface, and so on throughout the flyer until nearly every line of type has its own point size. This approach obliterates a clear hierarchy.

Another example might be planning the sizes for a number of charts to be included in a report. You may feel that the information in the charts covers a range of information of greater or lesser importance. You decide to try to show each chart at a size relative to the importance of the information it conveys. If you have eight different charts and plan to show them at eight different sizes over several pages, your hierarchy will

Create only the number of visually distinct levels you need. In this flyer the designer has tried to put each item on a different visual level by using different fonts, sizes, and weights. The result is too many levels that fight for the reader's attention. Nothing is distinct and consequently nothing is emphasized.

AdWorld Show Special
AdBudget
Finance Management Software for Advertising Agencies
Compare our features to any other software package! You'll get:
- • Media placement • Client billing
- • Production cost tracking

all handled automatically with AdBudget. AdBudget has it all.

Get AdBudget NOW for the Special AdWorld Show Price of only $289

See us at AdWorld Booth 342

dissolve—you reader will not see the pattern. Instead, he will assume the charts have been printed at random sizes. It would be better to settle on two or at most three sizes for the charts and to decide for each chart if it should be large, medium, or small.

In general, aim for fewer rather than more levels: The fewer the levels, the easier it is for each to be distinct, and the easier it is for your reader to grasp the organization of your document.

Make each level of your hierarchy of attention clearly different from the others. Don't create headlines that are "almost" the same size, photos or charts that are

By using only a few fonts, sizes and weights, this layout creates only the needed levels of attention. Each level is clear and the items that are meant to draw attention—such as the product name and the price—stand out.

AdWorld Show Special

AdBudget

Finance Management Software for Advertising Agencies

Compare our features to any other software package! You'll get:

- **Media placement**
- **Client billing**
- **Production cost tracking**

all handled automatically with AdBudget. AdBudget has it all.

Get AdBudget NOW for the Special AdWorld Show Price of only

$289

See us at AdWorld Booth 342

"nearly" equal, or blocks of white spaces that are "just about" the same. As much as you can, make each visual element match the others on its level, and make each level distinct.

Make sure font sizes are noticeably different. Don't combine headlines that are within a few point sizes of each other; this will make the hierarchy unclear. Remember that as a font becomes larger, the value of a single point becomes a smaller percentage of its size. For example, an 11-point font looks much larger than a 9-point font because it's more than 20 percent larger, but the difference between a 50-point font and a 52-

Make similar items look similar. In this layout similar parts of the message haven't been placed to show their relationship. Instead, the charts and pictures were spread through the story in a mistaken attempt to "break up" the text.

Harding Industries Acquires Nascom

The Electronic Giant Diversifies

In September, 1994, recalls James Harding, chief executive of the electronic giant Harding Industries, sales had gone south. Already under pressure from hundreds of new players in the volatile video game market, Harding had nothing to lose by taking a big new risk. "It was frightening," Harding recalls, "but there was nothing else to do. And it's turned out well so far."

Shareholders Earnings

The fearful time paid off. Harding surprised everyone—including Wall Street—with a first-quarter profit of $3.5 million. Many attribute that to the CEO's canny acquisition of Nascom earlier in the year.

In September, 1994, recalls James Harding, chief executive of the electronic giant Harding Industries, sales had gone south. Already under pressure from hundreds of new players in the volatile video

Don Oliver

game market, Harding had nothing to lose by taking a big new risk. "It was frightening," Harding recalls, "but there was nothing else to do. And it's turned out well so far."

CEO James Harding

The fearful time paid off. Harding surprised everyone—including Wall Street—with a first-quarter profit of $3.5 million. Many attribute that to the CEO's canny acquisition of Nascom earlier in the year.

In September, 1994, recalls James Harding, chief executive of the electronic giant Harding Industries, sales had gone south. Already under pressure from hundreds of new players in the volatile video game market,

Pat Hastings

Harding had nothing to lose by taking a big new risk. "It was frightening," Harding recalls, "but there was nothing else to do. And it's turned out well so far."

The fearful time paid off. Harding surprised everyone—including Wall Street—with a first-quarter profit of $3.5 million. Many attribute that to the CEO's canny acquisition of Nascom earlier in the year.

In September, 1994, recalls James Harding, chief executive of the electronic giant Harding Industries, sales had gone south. Already under pressure from hundreds of new players in the volatile video game market, Harding had nothing to lose by tak-

ing a big new risk. "It was frightening," Harding recalls, "but there was nothing else to do. And it's turned out well so far."

The fearful time paid off. Harding surprised everyone—including Wall Street—with a first-quarter profit of $3.5 million. Many attribute that to the CEO's canny acquisition of Nascom earlier in the year.

In September, 1994, recalls James

Quarterly Profit

Harding, chief executive of the electronic giant Harding Industries, sales had gone south. Already under pressure from hundreds of new players in the volatile video game market, Harding had nothing to lose by taking a big new risk. "It was frightening," Harding recalls, "but there was nothing else to do. And it's turned out well so far."

The fearful time paid off. Harding surprised everyone—including Wall Street—with a first-quarter profit of $3.5 million. Many attribute that to the CEO's canny acquisition of Nascom earlier in the year.

In September, 1994, recalls James Harding, chief executive of the electr

point font is only 4 percent—not enough to be clearly seen. As a rule, make sure that there is at least a 10 percent size difference between any two fonts you are using in a single document.

If you have used position as part of your hierarchy, be consistent, or you will inadvertently create an extra level in your hierarchy. For example, if you're using heads of the same level that align left, align them all to the left—don't center some and not others. If the description that accompanies your first chart's is below the chart, don't put the next chart's description above the chart.

Here the people and numbers have been gathered into two similar-looking boxes, which helps readers understand that they are two components of the larger story of the acquisition.

Harding Industries Acquires Nascom

The Electronic Giant Diversifies

In September, 1994, recalls James Harding, chief executive of the electronic giant Harding Industries, sales had gone south. Already under pressure from hundreds of new players in the volatile video game market, Harding had nothing to lose by taking a big new risk. "It was frightening," Harding recalls, "but there was nothing else to do. And it's turned out well so far."

The fearful time paid off. Harding surprised everyone—including Wall Street—with a first-quarter profit of $3.5 million. Many attribute that to the CEO's canny acquisition of Nascom earlier in the year.

In September, 1994, recalls James Harding, chief executive of the electronic giant Harding Industries, sales had gone south. Already under pressure from hundreds of new players in the volatile video game market, Harding had nothing to lose by taking a big new risk. "It was frightening," Harding recalls, "but there was nothing else to do. And it's turned out well so far."

The fearful time paid off. Harding

surprised everyone—including Wall Street—with a first-quarter profit of $3.5 million. Many attribute that to the CEO's canny acquisition of Nascom earlier in the year.

The Numbers

Shareholders earnings **Quarterly Profit**

In September, 1994, recalls James Harding, chief executive of the electronic giant Harding Industries, sales had gone south. Already under pressure from hundreds of new players in the volatile video game market, Harding had nothing to lose by taking a big new risk. "It was frightening," Harding recalls, "but there was nothing else to do. And it's turned

out well so far."

The fearful time paid off. Harding surprised everyone—including Wall Street—with a first-quarter profit of $3.5 million. Many attribute that to

the CEO's canny acquisition of Nascom earlier in the year.

In September, 1994, recalls James Harding, chief executive of the electronic giant Harding Industries, sales had gone south. Already under pressure from hundreds of new players in the volatile video game market, Harding had nothing to lose by taking a big new risk. "It was frightening," Harding recalls, "but there was nothing else to do. And it's turned out well so far."

The fearful time paid off. Harding surprised everyone—including Wall Street—with a first-quarter profit of $3.5 million. Many attribute that to the CEO's canny acquisition of Nascom earlier in the year.

In September, 1994, recalls James Harding, chief executive of the electronic giant Harding Industries, sales had gone south. Already under pres

The People

CEO James Harding **Pat Hastings** **Don Oliver**

---

26. Make similar items look similar.

When your reader sees two items that look alike, he will assume their content is alike in some way. By taking advantage of this assumption, you can make items appear similar to show that they are part of a set. For example, if your document is divided into sections, each section's headline should be the same font and size. Each subhead should also be the same font and size, as should all the captions.

Magazine designers use this principle by making the recurring sections of the magazine—letters to the editor, product reviews, or news briefs, for example—look similar. By seeing the same font and layout for all the departments, a reader understands (perhaps subconsciously) that these sections are part of a set—the set of recurring sections—and not feature stories. Regular columns by staff writers may have yet another consistent style.

You can use this principle in business documents as well. If you are producing an employee newsletter and have information that appears regularly (for example, an employee of the month story), use the same design format each time it appears. In a brochure that features photographs of several products, make the photos the same size.

Because people assume this similarity between items that look the same, you can use this principle to control a reader's perception. Let's say your company has for years consisted of three large, stable divisions. A new division has just been created, one that is small and inexperienced, yet you know that it is this division's work that will most impress a potential client you are trying to capture. In your proposal, you can make each of the four divisions appear equal by designing a proposal with four sections on the four divisions—each of which has the same size headline and same amount of space. The impression will be that the company is equally divided between the four divisions, as is the document.

27. Organize your material into simple shapes.

When you are designing a multicolumn document, you will often have a number of different visual elements on the same page. Each of these elements creates a shape of some kind. Columns of type are usually rectangles, as are photos, charts, and graphs, while headlines can either be arranged in groups that create shapes or can stand alone, showing the shapes of the individual words. The content of a photograph—a face, a crowd, a car—creates shapes as well. Illustrations and graphic elements often create irregular shapes. And the unprinted parts (the white space) create shapes. Item by item, you need to consider and control these shapes, bringing them together to form new, simple shapes, because a page with a few simple shapes will be understood more quickly than a busy page.

If you're working with a photograph, chart, or illustration, consider how busy or simple it looks. If it has a lot of shapes within it, showing it large will make it easier to see the detail clearly. Make the rest of the layout simple, so the reader can concentrate his efforts studying the detail. If you've got a simple photo—a portrait, for example—your layout can be more complex. Remember, though, that there's nothing wrong with a simple photo that's combined with a simple layout. Advertisers use the "big photo, big headline, block of body copy" layout over and over again—and with good result. This kind of layout communicates the message very quickly. But busy pictures in a busy layout make a confusing mess.

Arrange your items—blocks of body copy, photos, charts, headlines, boxes and white space—the way you would pack a suitcase. What items fit neatly next to each other? In packing, you put what you'll need first on top; in a layout, put what your reader needs first on top (or emphasize it in some other way—see Rule 24). Just as you might fold a sweater to make it smaller, or decide to leave it out, you might reduce the size of a photo or eliminate it altogether.

Try to combine items so that they create one simple shape—usually a square or rectangle, or combine them so that the white space that remains is a simple shape.

Organize your material into simple shapes. In this layout, each of the items—the pictures, the headline and the text—have been put on the page so that each takes on its own shape. Not only does this create a number of random shapes on the page (the centered headline is one example) but it also creates chunks of irregular white space between the items. All these shapes make it hard for the reader's eye to know where to look.

Quality research is a tradition at SourceTech

I n September, 1994, recalls James Harding, chief executive of the electronic giant Harding Industries, sales had gone south. Already under pressure from hundreds of new players in the volatile video game market, Harding had nothing to lose by taking a big new risk. "It was frightening," Harding recalls, "but there was nothing else to do. And it's turned out well so far."

The fearful time paid off. Harding surprised everyone—including Wall Street—with a first-quarter profit of $3.5 million. Many attribute that to the CEO's canny acquisition of Nascom earlier in the year.

In September, 1994, recalls James Harding, chief executive of the electronic giant Harding Industries, sales had

gone south. Already under pressure from hundreds of new players in the volatile video game market, Harding had nothing to lose by taking a big new risk. "It was frightening," Harding recalls, "but there was nothing else to do. And it's turned out well so far."

The fearful time paid off. Harding surprised everyone—including Wall Street—with a first-quarter profit of $3.5 million. Many attribute that to the CEO's canny acquisition of Nascom earlier in the year.

In September, 1994, recalls James Harding, chief executive of the electronic giant Harding Industries, things were tough.

For example, if you have a lot of irregularly shaped drawings of products, you might want to top-align them with an imaginary line so that the space above them is a clear rectangle.

A word of caution about white space. When some people learn just enough about design to be dangerous, they often cry "put in more white space!" But adding white space just anywhere—in little blobs across the page, for example—can ruin a layout. White space should frame the elements or create a useful shape; otherwise it's a waste of paper.

Although you may hear otherwise, it isn't true that

In this layout the items have been gathered into a roughly half-circle shape. This also organizes the white space into a long rectangular band on the left and, on the right, a curved space that matches the half-circle. The result is a design that is much easier to visually comprehend.

Quality research is a tradition at SourceTech

In September, 1994, recalls James Harding, chief executive of the electronic giant Harding Industries, sales had gone south. Already under pressure from hundreds of new players in the volatile video game market, Harding had nothing to lose by taking a big new risk. "It was frightening," Harding recalls, "but there was nothing else to do. And it's turned out well so far."

The fearful time paid off. Harding surprised everyone—including Wall Street—with a first-quarter profit of $3.5 million. Many attribute that to the CEO's canny acquisition of Nascom earlier in the year.

In September, 1994, recalls James Harding, chief executive of the electronic giant Harding Industries, sales had gone south. Already under pressure from hundreds of new players in the volatile video

game market, Harding had nothing to lose by taking a big new risk. "It was frightening," Harding recalls, "but there was nothing else to do. And it's turned out well so far."

The fearful time paid off. Harding surprised everyone—including Wall Street—with a first-quarter profit of $3.5 million. Many attribute that to the CEO's canny acquisition of Nascom earlier in the year.

In September, 1994, recalls James Harding, chief executive of the electronic giant Harding Industries, things were tough.

text must be broken up with photos or charts. It's often better to break up the text with subheads, *dropcaps,* or *pullquotes* than with a graphic item. (Dropcaps are headline-sized letters that begin the first paragraph of a section; pullquotes are headline-sized quotes pulled from the story, often put in a box in the text). There is nothing wrong with grouping photos or charts together in their own spot away from the text. This usually makes the text easier to read and the illustrations easier to see. This isn't to say that you can never put a photo in a block of text—just that it's far from required.

Type in a column takes on the shape of the column,

To organize the shapes of your material you must see items as having an overall shape. Type makes different shapes depending on how large it is. Shown here is type set at three different sizes, with a gray area indicating the general shape the type makes on the page.

Quality

Quality research is a tradition at SourceTech

The fearful time paid off. Harding surprised everyone—including Wall Street—with a first-quarter profit of $3.5 million. Many attribute that to the CEO's canny acquisition of Nascom earlier in the year.

but as type gets bigger (for example a headline) it takes on its own shape. The single word "Apple," for instance, when set in large type, has an irregular shape created by the triangular <u>A</u>, and the ascenders and descenders of the lowercase letters. By seeing its shape, you can fit it into your layout with more precision. You could tuck a small word in the gaps above the two p's, using smaller type in all capitals. (Using all capitals keeps that word rectangular in shape, and fits well against the tops of the p's.) Or, if you wanted to disguise the shape of the word "Apple," you could put it in a box. The shape of the box would then be more prominent than the shape of the word.

When you use headline type in smaller sizes, the shape you create tends to be determined less by the shapes of the words and more by the shape of the block. For instance, three lines of headline type set flush left create a block with a straight left edge and a ragged right edge. When you use blocks of headline type, the aligning vertical line, whether it's the left edge, right edge, or through the center, should align with something else in the layout—this is one way to reduce the number of alignment lines and so simplify the shapes on your page.

One style of setting text, often used in letters and memos and occasionally in reports and advertisements, is to add space between paragraphs. If you use this style, don't add a full line space—that turns the paragraphs into floating blocks. A good rule of thumb is to add only half the line space value between lines. For example, a 10-point font set on 12 points of line space should have 6 extra points of line space between the paragraphs. And don't indent the first line of paragraphs that are separated by space—the space itself signals the beginning of each new paragraph; indenting the first line complicates the shape of the paragraphs for no reason.

For advanced designers, the most effective method to control and create shapes in a layout is to use a grid. A grid is an alignment system of evenly spaced horizontal and vertical guidelines you can use to align all the items in your layout: text blocks, headlines, photos, charts, and captions. The vertical lines of a grid are typically those of the text columns, although guidelines running through the columns may also be included. The horizontal lines usually bear a proportional relationship to the vertical columns. If you are designing a newsletter, magazine, or annual report, establishing a grid can be very helpful, although the details are beyond the scope of this book. For books that provide more information on grids, see the Bibliography.

Harding Industries Acquires Nascom

The Electronic Giant Diversifies

In September, 1994, recalls James Harding, chief executive of the electronic giant Harding Industries, sales had gone south. Already under pressure from hundreds of new players in the volatile video game market, Harding had nothing to lose by taking a big new risk. "It was frightening," Harding recalls, "but there was nothing else to do. And it's turned out well so far."

The fearful time paid off. Harding surprised everyone—including Wall Street—with a first-quarter profit of $3.5 million. Many attribute that to the CEO's canny acquisition of Nascom earlier in the year.

In September, 1994, recalls James Harding, chief executive of the electronic giant Harding Industries, sales had gone south. Already under pressure from hundreds of new players in the volatile video game market, Harding had nothing to lose by taking a big new risk. "It was frightening," Harding recalls, "but there was

surprised everyone—including Wall Street—with a first-quarter profit of $3.5 million. Many attribute that to the CEO's canny acquisition of Nascom earlier in the year.

The Numbers

Shareholders earnings   **Quarterly Profit**

In September, 1994, recalls James Harding, chief executive of the electronic giant Harding Industries, sales had gone south. Already under pressure from hundreds of new players in the volatile video game market, Harding had nothing to lose by tak-

The People

CEO James Harding   **Pat Hastings**   **Don Oliver**

nothing else to do. And it's turned out well so far."

The fearful time paid off. Harding

ing a big new risk. "It was frightening," Harding recalls, "but there was nothing else to do. And it's turned

out well so far."

The fearful time paid off. Harding surprised everyone—including Wall Street—with a first-quarter profit of $3.5 million. Many attribute that to

the CEO's canny acquisition of Nascom earlier in the year.

In September, 1994, recalls James Harding, chief executive of the electronic giant Harding Industries, sales had gone south. Already under pressure from hundreds of new players in the volatile video game market, Harding had nothing to lose by taking a big new risk. "It was frightening," Harding recalls, "but there was nothing else to do. And it's turned out well so far."

The fearful time paid off. Harding surprised everyone—including Wall Street—with a first-quarter profit of $3.5 million. Many attribute that to the CEO's canny acquisition of Nascom earlier in the year.

In September, 1994, recalls James Harding, chief executive of the electronic giant Harding Industries, sales had gone south. Already under pressure from hundreds of new players in

28. Arrange your text so that it's easy to follow.

In a single-column document, the path of the reader is straightforward, but in a multiple-column layout there is the possibility of blocking that path. If you are creating a multiple-column document, make sure you place the text on the page so that when your reader gets to the end of a column it's obvious where the story picks up again. This is easy to overlook when you're considering the page visually. The tendency is to see the columns of text as gray blocks that can be moved anywhere on the page. Designers have sometimes con-

Here the box has been moved to the bottom of the page so

Harding Industries Acquires Nascom

The Electronic Giant Diversifies

In September, 1994, recalls James Harding, chief executive of the electronic giant Harding Industries, sales had gone south. Already under pressure from hundreds of new players in the volatile video game market, Harding had nothing to lose by taking a big new risk. "It was frightening," Harding recalls, "but there was nothing else to do. And it's turned out well so far."

The fearful time paid off. Harding surprised everyone—including Wall Street—with a first-quarter profit of $3.5 million. Many attribute that to the CEO's canny acquisition of Nascom earlier in the year.

In September, 1994, recalls James Harding, chief executive of the electronic giant Harding Industries, sales had gone south. Already under pressure from hundreds of new players in the volatile video game market, Harding had nothing to lose by taking a big new risk. "It was frightening," Harding recalls, "but there was nothing else to do. And it's turned out well so far."

The fearful time paid off. Harding

surprised everyone—including Wall Street—with a first-quarter profit of $3.5 million. Many attribute that to the CEO's canny acquisition of Nascom earlier in the year.

The Numbers

Shareholders earnings

Quarterly Profit

In September, 1994, recalls James Harding, chief executive of the electronic giant Harding Industries, sales had gone south. Already under pressure from hundreds of new players in the volatile video game market, Harding had nothing to lose by taking a big new risk. "It was frightening," Harding recalls, "but there was nothing else to do. And it's turned

out well so far."

The fearful time paid off. Harding surprised everyone—including Wall Street—with a first-quarter profit of $3.5 million. Many attribute that to

the CEO's canny acquisition of Nascom earlier in the year.

In September, 1994, recalls James Harding, chief executive of the electronic giant Harding Industries, sales had gone south. Already under pressure from hundreds of new players in the volatile video game market, Harding had nothing to lose by taking a big new risk. "It was frightening," Harding recalls, "but there was nothing else to do. And it's turned out well so far."

The fearful time paid off. Harding surprised everyone—including Wall Street—with a first-quarter profit of $3.5 million. Many attribute that to the CEO's canny acquisition of Nascom earlier in the year.

In September, 1994, recalls James Harding, chief executive of the electronic giant Harding Industries, sales had gone south. Already under pres

The People

CEO James Harding

Pat Hastings

Don Oliver

tributed to this tendency by insisting that text blocks be broken up. Sometimes that's a good idea—but never at the expense of readability.

The problem usually occurs when you place a photo, chart, or some other graphic in the text path in a way that isolates a small part of the text near the bottom of the page. After a reader finishes a column, the natural tendency is to look up, not down, to find the rest of the story.

A better way to break up text is with dropcaps or *crossheads* (small but bold subheads, usually centered over the column). Crossheads work well in reports and

letters because they help the reader skim the information. Dropcaps are better in documents such as employee newsletters and annual reports. It has been found in advertising research that dropcaps increase readership by 13 percent.

29. Design a multipage or folded document as a sequence of scenes.

In multipage or folded documents, your reader experiences your message over time, as the pages are turned or the panels unfolded. Think of your document as being like a play: Each page corresponds to an act; each item on the page is a scene. You begin with act I, scene 1—and some part of your information is delivered. Scene 2 delivers more; then you move on to act II, Scene 1.

Thinking this way, you can see how all the items on the page should not be (and cannot be) of equal importance or excitement. Imagine a play where every scene is a battle scene—by the end, the members of the audience would be exhausted and confused (that is, if they actually stayed through the entire performance).

If your document will be mailed in an envelope, the envelope itself is the first act, and presents the first opportunity to start the flow of communication. You

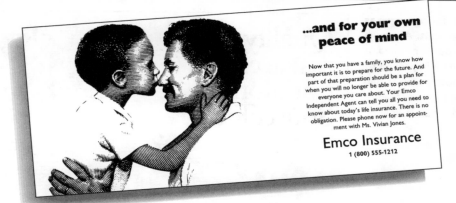

...and for your own peace of mind

Now that you have a family, you know how important it is to prepare for the future. And part of that preparation should be a plan for when you will no longer be able to provide for everyone you care about. Your Emco Independent Agent can tell you all you need to know about today's life insurance. There is no obligation. Please phone now for an appointment with Ms. Vivian Jones.

Emco Insurance
1 (800) 555-1212

Design a multipage or folded document as a sequence of scenes. The three-panel folded brochure shown above has been designed to draw readers in opening each panel to reveal more of the message. The first panel begins with an incomplete headline (indicated by the ellipses). Unfolding to the second panel, the reader sees a partially-covered illustration and another incomplete headline. Finally, by opening up the brochure all the way, the reader receives the full illustration and the sales text.

might put a provocative headline here to arouse a reader's curiosity, encouraging a look inside.

A folded brochure, because it becomes larger as it is unfolded, should consist of expanding scenes, each having greater impact than the one before. You can exploit this quality by building anticipation at each step. For example, you might show only partial views of a new product on each panel, culminating in a big photo of the entire product.

Be aware that everyone won't unfold a brochure the same way you would. Test your design by giving a mock-up to a few people, and watch how they unfold it. If they don't do it "correctly," either redesign it so there is only one way it can be unfolded or make each panel's information independent so the brochure makes sense no matter how it is unfolded.

A magazine is often arranged like a three-act play. The first section opens with letters to the editor, regular columns, and opinion pages; the middle section (often called the well) is reserved for features; the last section may finish with other regular columns, a calendar of events, and the continued parts of the features.

Within each section, a reader should know where he is and where he is going. Regular columns (in the beginning and ending sections) should look the same

so they are recognized when they occur (see Rule 26). Features should look dramatically different from regular columns, and each feature should have its own style.

30. Design facing pages as a single unit.

In magazine and newspaper design, two facing pages are called a *spread*. Because they are seen together, you can increase their impact if you design them as one visual presentation. In a folded brochure, any panels that are seen together are also a visual unit. In either case, think of creating a hierarchy of attention not for each separate page but for the entire spread (see Rule 24).

The fold or break between pages is a visual element that tends to divide a spread. (The margin between two facing pages or the space between two columns of type is called a *gutter*.) There are two ways to work with this element: first, try to disguise it, or second, incorporate it into your plan.

To disguise the break, use a large visual element horizontally to cross the gutter —a photo, illustration, or a large headline are best. Make sure that the break

By putting the headline across the center gutter, this layout visually unites both pages into a single presentation.

Quality research is a tradition at SourceTech

doesn't cut through the photo in a bad spot (splitting someone's face, for example) or cut through a block of text. Another technique is to put a line of boxed items, such as charts, across the top or bottom of both pages. Although nothing actually crosses the gutter in this case, the horizontal line of boxes visually overpowers the vertical break between pages.

To incorporate the break or fold into your layout, put two items on facing pages that relate to each other. Magazines commonly put a full-page photo on the left-hand page and the beginning of the article on the right. You might also design the left and right pages so that they match each other exactly, with photos, headlines, and text blocks in the same positions. In a brochure, you might want to devote one panel completely to a headline, and its accompanying panel to the text.

There will be many times when you won't be able to achieve an ideal design relationship between two pages because the material you're working with just won't cooperate. But if you're aware that the pages will be seen together, you can usually make some adjustments so that the two pages don't fight each other.

Quality research is a tradition at SourceTech

31. Keep live matter away from the edge of the paper and the gutter.

All the type and images that you want to appear on a page are traditionally called the *live matter*. In traditional printing, this term is used to distinguish this material from the part the printer will trim off. When you see a photograph in a magazine that runs all the way to the edge of a page, that effect (called *bleeding*) was created by printing on oversized paper and then trimming back to cut off part of the image. If you are designing a page and decide to bleed a photograph or illustration, make sure that the part of the image you want to stay on the page (the live matter of the photo) is at least a quarter of an inch away from the trim line.

If you're designing a multipage document that will be bound, you need to allow extra space on the binding edge of the page; otherwise part of your live matter will "fall into the gutter."

How much space you need depends on the kind of binding. If your document will be inserted in a three-ring binder, you should allow a full inch for the bind-

This layout corrects the problem by "flopping" the photos (see text) so that the people are looking inward.

Quality research is a tradition at SourceTech

ing side. If your document will have a square binding, either a glued binding by a professional printer (like paperback books, called *perfect binding*) or a binding produced by a sophisticated copy machine (which typically uses wire or head-sealed tape), you should leave at least three-quarters of an inch margin on the binding side. This dimension can change, however, depending on how thick your document will be—the thicker the document, the more margin you'll need.

If your document will be stapled down a center fold to create a letter-sized document such as a magazine (called *saddle stitching*) you can reduce this margin to a quarter-inch if necessary.

Aside from these practical considerations, generous margins help a document look inviting—type and photos that fill a page nearly edge to edge look cramped.

32. Face photos of people into the page.

This is an old rule, the idea being that a person pictured looking off the page will direct the reader's attention there as well.

If you're designing a two-page spread, people in the photos should be facing toward the center line created by the fold. On a single-page layout (such as a newsletter's front page), they should be facing an imaginary center line of the page that runs from top to bottom.

There are times, however, when you may not be able to place a photo so that the person is looking in. If you're sending your newsletter out to a printer, you can ask the printer to flop the photo's negative (that is, turn it over); some desktop publishing and scanning programs can accomplish this as well. This produces a mirror image of the photo and gets the person looking in the right direction. Be careful, though, because everything in the photo will be reversed. If there is lettering in the photo, it will be backwards; if there is a violinist, he will become left-handed; if there is a foreign flag on a wall, you may create an international incident. These situations, necessarily, override this rule.

In other cases it may simply look better to face a person off the page for dramatic effect—a visionary executive scanning distant horizons, for example.

33. Don't print photos of people in unusual ink colors.

If you're sending a document with photos out to be printed, and you have the budget for an added color, don't be tempted to print the photos in that color, especially those of people. Unless you can afford full-color reproduction, keep your photos black and white. Other colors draw attention to the color and not to what is pictured. Blue people look cold, green people look sickly, purple people look downright weird, and most other colors create similarly jarring effects. The one exception is some shades of brown, which create an old-time sepia look that is acceptable if that's the effect you're after.

34. Design coupons to be usable.

If your document includes a coupon, make sure it is convenient to use. When you're trying to squeeze information into a document, it's easy to create a coupon with lines that are too short or too close together to easily fill out, which defeats the purpose of providing a coupon. The space between lines in a coupon should be at least 24 points; more is even better. Coupons are also made more convenient by placing them near the edge of the page, so they can be cut out.

If you want a reader to keep information, don't put it on the back of a coupon; after it is sent, you'll have the information and your reader won't. If your document is to be mailed to your reader, a common plan is to arrange the coupon so it is on the reverse side of the mailing label. When a reader returns the coupon, his mailing address is on the back.

Also, make sure that the paper you're having your document printed on can be written on; some glossy papers used for printing are so slick that many pens won't write on them. Avoid shading a coupon; this also makes it harder for ink to stick to it.

35. Observe postal regulations.

If you are designing something that will be mailed, you must check with the post office to make sure your design will be accepted, unless your document will be mailed in a standard envelope.

If you decide to use text on the outside of the envelope anywhere except the usual return address corner, you must check with the post office. Many spaces on the front of an envelope are reserved for postal use.

If your document will be a self-mailer—that is, mailed without an envelope—find out the restrictions on dimensions, size, and folds. Some folded pieces must be stapled closed or sealed in some other way or the post office will refuse them.

Some document designs will be accepted by the post office but can only be mailed at a premium price. It is possible that you could design a mailer one-quarter of an inch too long in one dimension and find that to mail a large quantity will cost you hundreds of dollars extra for special handling.

Finally, it's important that when you ask about postal regulations, you ask at the post office from which you will be mailing your piece. Postal regulations are voluminous, complex, and subject to interpretation. What one post office will accept will be turned down flat by another.

36. Don't overdesign.

A lot of decoration can be added to a document that provides no increase in communication at all. Don't be tempted to put in lines, boxes, tints, or anything else unless the item helps communicate your message. Lines can divide two sections of information that might otherwise run together, boxes can group common items and show that they are part of a set, and tints can highlight information, increasing its contrast and so raising it in the hierarchy of attention (see Rule 24). However, if these items will not be doing a job, don't add them.

When you're finished with your layout, look carefully for any added decoration that isn't helping you make your ideas clear. If you find one, eliminate it.

There is a story that illustrates this point. A respected jazz guitarist once sat in on a song with a young player. The older guitarist played beautifully, giving the tune an evocative quality that stirred the emotions with every note. The young player, determined to hold his own against the master, demonstrated his lightning speed and amazing technique, cleverly pushing the melody far beyond its original path. By the end of the performance, the young man was proud of himself, and wondered if he hadn't shown up the master. The older player turned to him and said, "You play the guitar well." The young man thanked him for the compliment. Then the master smiled, and continued, "But that's the difference between us. You play the guitar. I play the song."

Document Checklist

THE EASIEST WAY to get in the habit of following the rules in this book is to use a checklist for each document you create. On the facing page is a list of the rules with a checkbox next to each rule, along with the page number on which you can find a full explanation.

You can make copies of the list and then, when you design your next document, check off each rule as you consider or complete it. If you can't remember the rule's details, turn to the page indicated.

If you review documents created by others, you can use the checklist in another way: clip a checklist to the document with items checked that could be improved.

Looking Good on Paper Document Checklist

Glossary

ascender The part of a lowercase letter that extends above the x-height.

baseline The imaginary line on which lowercase letters sit.

bleed A printed image that runs to the very edge of the page; created by printing on oversized paper and then trimming off part of the image.

call for reaction That part of your message that indirectly asks your reader to believe something, such as the idea that your product is the best on the market.

call to action That part of your message that asks your reader to do something, such as call a phone number or send in a coupon.

color (of type) The quality of darkness or lightness that text type has as a large block of text type.

continuous tone The gray shades of a photograph before it has been prepared for printing.

crop To indicate a part of a photo or illustration that should not be printed, using crop marks on the edge of the image.

crosshead A small heading, usually bold, centered, and the same size as the text, that interrupts a column of type to begin a subsection.

descender The part of a lowercase letter that falls below the baseline.

dropcap A headline-sized capital letter that is set into the beginning of a paragraph of type to indicate a new section, usually extending two or three lines deep.

em-space A unit of measurement equal to the width of the uppercase letter *M* in a given font.

en-space A unit of measurement equal to the width of the uppercase letter *N* in a given font; also equal to half of an em-space.

flush left, flush right Aligning text so that either the left side or the right side, respectively, is even, and the other side is uneven.

grid An invisible structure made up of vertical column lines and horizontal lines to help arrange a layout.

gutter The margin between two facing pages; also the space between two columns of type.

halftone The result of preparing a continuous-tone photograph for printing—that is, changing it into a pattern of small black-and-white dots.

hierarchy of attention The order into which the visual components of a layout are arranged, using the qualities of size, contrast, position, form, and content.

justified Text alignment that is even on both the left and right sides.

kerning The adjustment of space between two particular characters, often measured in tenths or hundredths of an em-space.

kerning pair Two characters that must be kerned—for example, some common kerning pairs are AT, WA, FA, VA, LT, Ta, Te, Yo, and Ye.

leader dots A line of dots from one item in a column to the next, commonly found in a phone listing or table of contents.

leading See line space.

left-justified Flush left alignment.

letterspace The amount of space between letters, usually measured in points or fractions of points.

line space The amount of space between lines of type, usually measured in points.

live matter All the images and text that are to remain on the page, as opposed to being trimmed off, as in a bleed.

moiré pattern An undesirable cross-hatch pattern that occurs when a halftone photograph is screened again.

perfect binding A glued binding with a square spine, used on paperback books.

pica A measurement used in publication design, especially for the width of a column of type, consisting of 12 points. There are approximately six picas to an inch.

point A measurement used in publication design, especially for font size, line spacing, and sometimes for letterspacing. There are approximately 72 points to an inch.

pullquote A part of the text which is "pulled" and enlarged to headline size, usually put in a box and used as a graphic element to break up a page of text.

rag right, rag left Flush left and flush right alignment, respectively.

right-justified Flush right alignment.

river An undesirable channel of white space running through a column of type, caused by poor word spacing.

saddle stitching A binding method using stapling along the center fold of a publication, common in magazines.

screening The traditional process of preparing a continuous-tone photograph for printing, which creates a halftone.

serif The finishing stroke of a letter, such as the two serifs on the ends of the crossbar of the letter *T*.

spread Two pages or panels of a publication seen at the same time.

stem The main upright stroke of a letter.

tint A shade of color, often black, created by using a small dot pattern and expressed in a percentage; a 10 percent tint is very light; a 90 percent tint is very dark.

word space The space between words, often measured in tenths or hundredths of an em-space.

x-height The height of lowercase letters, as determined by the lowercase *x*, usually measured in fractions of an Em-space.

Selected Bibliography

In my opinion, most books that try to offer advice on document design consist of little more than a disorganized collection of tips, which are sometimes useful in the particular situation illustrated, but often not. The few books I recommend below don't suffer from that flaw. Each of them has a strong viewpoint and contains information that can be applied to a broad range of publications.

Editing by Design, **Jan White** (New York & London: R. R. Bowker, 1974). To my mind, this is the classic book on the layout of multipage documents, particularly magazines. White analyzes the visual properties of fonts, column arrangement, photographs, and graphs, among other things, and offers an excellent introduction to using a grid. Essential reading for anyone who will be designing a newsletter, magazine, or annual report.

The Grid, **Allen Hurlburt** (New York: Van Nostrand Reinhold, 1982). For those involved in producing multipage documents in which a large variety of items will be used, nothing is better for organizing a layout than a grid, and no book is better at explaining how to create and use grids than Hurlburt's. This former art director for *Look* magazine uses both simple and complex grids to produce elegant and striking results.

***Ogilvy on Advertising*, David Ogilvy** (New York: Crown, 1983). As no-nonsense a book on advertising as you are likely to find, and one that's fun to read as well. Ogilvy is legendary in the advertising business, and as opinionated as they come. His advice is definite, concrete, and applicable to nearly anything you will be putting on paper that is intended to persuade. Highly recommended.

***Type from the Desktop*, Clifford Burke** (Chapel Hill, North Carolina: Ventana Press, 1990). If, on the basis of my brief introduction, you have become fascinated by typography, this is an excellent book to pursue an education in type. Burke is well grounded in traditional knowledge, yet the book is directed toward those who use today's desktop publishing systems.

***Age of Propaganda: The Everyday Use and Abuse of Persuasion*, Anthony Pratkanis and Elliot Aronson** (New York: W. H. Freeman and Company, 1992). Although this book is not about design, it is essential reading for anyone interested in the persuasion process. Written by two psychology professors, the book covers persuasion techniques used by everyone from politicians to sales people.

About the Author

GARRETT SODEN has worked for more than twenty years as a writer, publication designer, and communications specialist. During his seven years as an administrator for Occidental College, he taught editorial design to student interns. He was most recently Director of Corporate Communications for Commuter Transportation Services, Inc., in Los Angeles.

As an editorial design consultant, he has worked for the Los Angeles County Bar Association, the Los Angeles chapter of the Anti-Defamation League, and the California Credit Union League, among others, and has acted as a desktop publishing trainer for employees of the Claremont Graduate School. He has given seminars on desktop publishing for the Public Relations Association of Southern California Colleges and the Council for Advancement and Support of Education.

Now a full-time writer, Mr. Soden is also the author of *I Went to College for This? True Stuff About the Business World—And How to Make Your Way Through It*, a career guide for recent graduates, and *Hook, Spin, Buzz: The Art of Business Communication in the Age of Information Overload*. Mr. Soden is also the coauthor of a humor book entitled *The One Minute Maniac*.

Mr. Soden lives in Pasadena, California, with his wife, artist Denise K. Seider, their daughter, Jordan Seider, and Tom the Cat.

Design Notes